Rivers, Ridges, and Valleys

Essays on Rural Pennsylvania

Edited by
Jerry Wemple &
Anne Dyer Stuart

an imprint of Sunbury Press, Inc.
Mechanicsburg, PA USA

an imprint of Sunbury Press, Inc.
Mechanicsburg, PA USA

FIRST CATAMOUNT PRESS EDITION: February 2025

Set in Adobe Garamond Pro | Interior design by Crystal Devine | Cover by Lawrence Knorr | Edited by Gabrielle Kirk.

Publisher's Cataloging-in-Publication Data
Names: Jerry Wemple, et al.
Title: Rivers, ridges, and valleys : essays on rural Pennsylvania.
Description: First trade paperback edition. | Mechanicsburg, PA : Catamount Press, 2025.
Summary: With its diverse history and landscapes—from farmland and vast woods to coal mines and mill towns—rural Pennsylvania defies easy description. The essays of the twenty-seven contributors to *Rivers, Ridges, and Valleys* deftly illuminate often overlooked facets of the Keystone State.
Identifiers: ISBN : 979-8-88819-304-4 (softcover).
Subjects: LITERARY COLLECTIONS / Essays | LITERARY COLLECTIONS / Subjects & Themes / Places | SOCIAL SCIENCE / Sociology / Rural.

Designed in the USA
0 1 1 2 3 5 8 13 21 34 55

For the Love of Books!

Contents

Introduction

Here is a secret. Though my colleagues and friends associate me with Pennsylvania, I am a bit of a fraud. It is true that I can spout tons of PA trivia: Kennett Square is the mushroom capital of the world, Sunbury is home of the world's largest inflatable dam, Mount Davis in Somerset County is the highest spot in the state with an elevation of 3,213 feet. While I possess this arcane knowledge and genuine affection for the Keystone State, I spent a large chunk of my youth, from ages nine to sixteen, living in Florida. However, the entire time I lived in Florida, I felt like I was in exile. There was some deep-seated link between me and Pennsylvania. Trying to get a sense of "home," one autumn when I was ten or eleven and longing for the vibrant colors of the hills along the Susquehanna Valley, I asked my grandmother to send me some leaves. When the envelope arrived with brittle and nearly colorless remnants, they only deepened my longing, a symbol of what I was missing.

As a young man, I made my way in the world. Over the years, I lived in several other states, traveled coast to coast and to fourteen countries. Yet I always considered Pennsylvania, especially small-town Central PA, my home. Whenever I ran into someone in the region, we would usually fall in thick as thieves. When I was in the Navy and on a ship in the Indian Ocean, I met a guy from Snyder County, located across the river from my hometown of Sunbury. I could tell where Randy was from by his distinctive slow, drawn-out pronunciation of the letters *u* and *o,* typical of "country kids" from that area. We became good friends the rest of the time we were stationed together. When I was a reporter in Massachusetts, I met the owner of a traveling carnival set up as part of the local fair one summer. His Harrisburg accent betrayed him. After we talked for a while, he instructed his manager to give me carte blanche, anything I wanted on the carnival grounds.

It was always good to make those connections. As an adult, I lived out of state for twenty years, but I was never away for long. I'd visit two or three times a year, for a few days or up to a month once or twice. Through happenstance, I've been back in PA for over twenty years, living only a few miles from the farm my great-grandfather once owned and the first house I lived in as a child. As I write this, the last leaves, only a couple of weeks ago exhibiting the bright colors I sought long ago in Florida, are slipping from the trees on the ridge along the river. We Pennsylvanians understand the cycle and know they will be back in due time.

Whether we are native born or have come to settle in Pennsylvania, there is something in the state that seeps into us, that becomes part of us. This collection contains twenty-seven essays. The contributors are all established writers with a variety of publishing credits, and through their writing readers can feel their connection to the rivers, ridges, and valleys of the state. The writers vary in age, representing a couple of generations. About two-thirds are native Pennsylvanians. Those who came to the state came from places as wide ranging as Ohio, North Carolina, Utah, California, and the Philippines. There are several essays dealing with environmental issues such as the aftermath of coal mining and more recent hydraulic fracturing. Some essays celebrate the outdoors whether the adventure is in a backyard or an isolated trout stream. Other essays deal with family legacy and loss, and still others focus on the history of people and places. The essays all have a strong sense of place and represent rural areas in the north, south, east, and west of the state. It is my hope that you will enjoy reading them and learn, as I have, even more about the commonwealth.

Jerry Wemple
Bloomsburg, 2024

CHARISSE BALDORIA

Elements

In August, billows of green rise with tufts of rust and gold. We're headed to the town park but encounter the river instead, where mountains and trees grow from hazy, inverted versions of themselves, a vision that stretches left and right as we march like converts toward the bank.

It is 2012. My husband Dave and I have just moved to Bloomsburg, a small Pennsylvania town in the Ridge and Valley Appalachians, where I accepted a one-year position to teach piano at the university. We've never lived in the countryside before and I feel more at ease getting lost in a foreign city than in a forest which I imagine will swallow me whole.

A tree clings to land's edge but curves down toward the mirror, crowding the frame. It doesn't look like water; it's not blue, unlike the seas surrounding the island where I was born. Or maybe it's blue in parts, depending on where you look. As we get closer to the bank, the sky reveals its waterborne self, a stealthy sea.

Our one-year stay will turn into more than ten. A decade later, I will tell my friends that when I die, I want my ashes spread in three places: the Susquehanna River in Bloomsburg, the woods behind our garden not too far away, and the coral reefs in Anilao, Philippines, just sixty miles from where I was born and where I used to scuba-dive. Bloomsburg scores two out of three: an accomplishment for an adopted home.

But at this moment, there are no thoughts of death, no commitments to a place, no fears of getting lost.

No screaming in my veins as when an old man seated on a bench facing the river will yell "Charlie!" to Dave years later, and Dave, a Filipino like me but born in America, will explain that it's a derogatory term for an Asian person: short for "Victor Charlie" or "Viet Cong." I'm not yet about to rush to confront the man, and Dave will not yet hold me back to say we should keep our heads down.

We haven't yet lain down on a mat looking up to treetops and the sky or slept in a hammock we tied to trees by the water, oblivious of the world. We haven't seen concerts at the park with friends who will leave or paddled down the river feeling like we've entered the mouth of God.

Now, we stand on the cusp between river and land, restlessness and arrival. The mountains, the sky, and their shadow selves glimmer in the evening sun transmuting our bronze skin into copper. We breathe, take it in, and release.

Simply, we vow to return.

***

In its several-hundred-million-year life, I know I'm not the only one the Susquehanna River has enthralled. I imagine the giant-armed tyrannosaurs, colossal duck-billed dinosaurs, and armored nodosaurs feeding along the rivers of Cretaceous Appalachia whose mountains had, by then, eroded to almost a plain from their Himalayan heights a hundred million years back. And after the earth's secret motions uplifted the sloping fields over the millions of years that followed, after ice sheets marched and melted, the first peoples roamed and settled along the rejuvenated river for millennia before White colonists took over its banks and established their towns.

I haven't found many Filipino settlers here though I've recently discovered some: a woman from Manila who came in the 60s when her White husband became a professor; a woman from Pangasinan who, at sixteen, married a serviceman in a U.S. base and moved here in the 70s, to his parents' home; a couple from Iloilo who relocated from New York in the 80s to work and raise a family; and more recently, a woman from Nevada who married my husband's co-worker and now lives in their countryside compound.

I don't know all their languages. The Philippines, with its 7,600 islands, has at least 130 languages, forty of which are dying. I speak only the national language (Tagalog) and write in a colonial one (English). My husband, one-hundred percent Filipino by blood, speaks and writes only in English. He was born in Connecticut to an Ibanag mother and Pangasinense father who speak Tagalog to each other because they don't know each other's languages, even if they're from the same large island. They wanted Dave and his brother to fit in so they spoke only English to them.

English may very well be the language that unites us all. Though our brown bodies were not born in this valley or descended from its original peoples or its colonists, though we did not grow up in the farmlands or coal country and our forebears didn't fight in the American Revolution or Civil War, it is a place where we have begun, where we begin again, this meeting place of mountain and river older than the supercontinent of Pangea.

* * *

In Tagalog mythology, it is said that a Charon-like figure ferries the soul of the dead across a river to the other shore, where the sun drowns every evening. But where does this river go? From where does it originate?

I imagine the river as an artist: how it shapes the earth, cuts into ancient bedrock, deepens faults and folds, sculpts edges, and splits mountains as it strives to find the sea. It even transfigures the sky.

Equipped with an inflatable kayak and buoyant spirits, we go on the Susquehanna's voyage in microscale: a forty-five-minute leisurely paddle from one park to the next. We pump up the tandem kayak in seven minutes; at the end, we deflate it, roll it up, and throw it in the back of our car. On the water, we sometimes imagine we're Viking conquerors or Amazon adventurers encircled by piranhas. Real-life bald eagles and blue herons occasionally make an appearance but on a typical day, we listen to birdsong and row with a family of geese.

One late summer evening, not ready to break our post-dinner ritual, we set ourselves on the river on a race against the vanishing sun when swirls and eddies of strawberry, orange, lemon, and lavender spill like a sunset under out boat. We glide as if on glass, fling ripples on a mirror that never breaks. Like fingers, our paddles caress a sky of silk; they rise and fall with the river's breath. There are no other boats in sight, no other breaths. Is the river dreaming and are we in its thoughts? Or is this what it looks like after death?

We have stumbled upon a secret; no one was supposed to know. Above us is a watercolor haze but with us is the sun-spilled sky, bright and clear.

***

This improvised song will never be heard again though there will be more sunsets, more singing, more nights. It is dark by the time we end our journey at the town park, a stone's throw from the site of eighteenth-century Lenape settlements and of Fort McClure that colonists built during the Indian War. The Lenape must have paddled in canoes of hollowed trees, glided past these walls of woods and mountains softened by the river's face. How many meetings have taken place on these banks? How many wars?

On weekends, when we start earlier, we have a picnic at the end of our ride then lay on a mat facing the sky. Sometimes I go alone when Dave is at work. I lean against a tree and I read and write. I am drawn into the water, the words "perfect" and "content" pooling inside, penetrating the rocks of my bones. When I'm on or by the river, I want nothing else.

It may not be a coincidence then: my Tagalog ancestors were riverine. *Tagalog* likely originates from *taga-ilog*, people of the river. Towns in the ancient Tagalog kingdom were built along the Pasig River: Maynila, Sapa, Tondo. After Spain conquered Maynila in 1571, they built a fort where the kingdom's fort already stood, along the river's mouth that opened to a bay. America, too, will raise its flag here 327 years later, leading to almost 400 years of continued foreign rule.

***

I grew up in Quezon City, Philippines, in a tropical valley near Manila, just west of a fault line and a river. It lies on the Pacific Ring of Fire, home to three-quarters of the world's active volcanoes, origin of nearly all its earthquakes. It's like a Pennsylvanian summer year-round, only hotter and stickier. We have two seasons: rainy and dry. In the dry season, it doesn't rain as much.

The fault by my childhood home is locked, bound. Its last release was in 1771, while Pennsylvania was fighting for an independent America and the Philippines was a captive of Spain. Its confinement has forced it to store stress—until it no longer can. One day it will break. One day, the apocalypse will come home.

I am shocked to discover that there are two fault lines around Bloomsburg. When Africa collided with North America around three-hundred million years ago, the crust crumpled into the Appalachian Mountains and these faults likely formed. But as the continents spread, their restive temperaments were stilled. Now, their presence is merely inferred through sheets of sediment that are "out of order," through exposed layers of tightly folded rocks. Will they reawaken, like the return of the dark lord to an unsuspecting Middle-earth? We might have to wait several hundred million years to find out.

Our first Bloomsburg home was on a mountain. On the western slope of Turkey Hill, near Bloomsburg's highest point, our apartment lay against a slope of sandstone and shale: remnants of Appalachia's oceanic past when it was submerged under a shallow sea. The sun crept up from behind blushing ridges and set conifer crowns ablaze before it disappeared. The Catawissa Mountain always dominated the scene, framed by another curving tree bowing to the sky. It's a view I never tired of. When composing, I used to turn sideways from the piano as if to take dictation from outdoors. It gave me a crick in the neck.

Mountain and river are my twin fixations, I soon discovered; I found myself captive to both in New Zealand's South Island where much of *Lord of the Rings* was filmed. After my alpine adventures in Middle-earth, Bloomsburg was simply the Shire and the magnificent Catawissa Mountain no more than a mound.

But the Shire has a charm all its own, even if our area's inhabitants look more like giants than hobbits. After hiking around the waterfalls at Ricketts Glen up on the Appalachian plateau where leaves have just started to turn, we drive valleyward past a big sign that says "Pig roast today."

Filipinos love pig roasts. One of my earliest memories was of a whole pig stretched across the dining table with an apple in its mouth. Dead and roasted, of course, its skin browned to crisp perfection. I am starved.

Dave makes a U-turn. Following the signs, we park in front of a barn. Dave's old Toyota Camry stands out from the trucks, bales of hay, and cowboy hats. It looks like a private party, not a festival as we'd assumed. "I feel awkward," I tell Dave who starts to back up. "Wait! All the more I want to stay!"

A man walks up and welcomes us to the fold. It's a fund-raising party for his twelve-year-old girl who is going to a wrestling camp. "It's five dollars and you can eat all you want!"

We pay the fee, help ourselves to the buffet, and go for the prize. Instead of a pig on a spit, we find one all neatly chopped up—it would have to do. We amble toward a picnic table, say hi to everyone we pass. An old man with a friendly drawl and NRA cap sits with us with his wife. We chat to the twang of Willie Nelson who the DJ plays all afternoon. While we munch on succulent pig meat and skin that remind us of *lechon*, he regales us with tales of his dog GW (the former President is to blame) and the black child they recently adopted ("He's very polite," he points out).

A young man sidles up to talk about guns. The host, gregarious like a town mayor, comes up to chat. The man with the NRA cap is his father and the "mayor" has eight children, four of whom we get to meet, wrestler included.

Five dollars seems a small price to pay for this experience so we walk over to the auction and splurge twenty. I notice cows roaming in the distance, the fields and mountains locked in a loose embrace. I am warmed by the openness, enjoy the spark that comes when different lives and landscapes meet and touch, even if spurred by the shared appreciation of roasted swine.

After Trump's election three years later, there'd be no way we'd ever crash a pig roast again.

***

Two soldiers who fought in the Philippine-American War, which resulted in 775,000 Filipino deaths, died of dysentery before their scheduled return to Bloomsburg in 1900. A Protestant missionary, who attempted to convert Muslims in southern Philippines and teach them to read and write their own language, has diaries in our university library. A friend who spent a few years in the Philippines as a child fondly remembers her Filipino nanny. These are area folks I've discovered with Philippine connections other than a spouse.

***

"Our home needs to have a mountain view," I assert. My one-year-position was converted to tenure-track, and eventually, I earned tenure. But the move away from our mountainside apartment we call "The Highlands" would be eight years in the making as we battled fears of job loss and our own fussiness. "Our new house must agree with Feng Shui principles, meaning no cul-de-sacs, no entry doors that open to stairs, no L-shaped houses . . ." And so on. The classical elements must be in balance at home; ch'i must move freely and energize the space. We needed all the help we could get.

We decide to build, thinking no existing house could possibly meet all our "needs." Fascinated by what is old yet fond of the new, I design a colonial-style house, a wannabe architect attempting to incorporate into Anglo-American tradition new technologies and principles of Feng Shui. We didn't want to be far from the town or river, but it shouldn't be too close to the river either due to flooding. Though the country lots had beautiful views, they frightened me: not only would I have to give up my sporty sedan so I could go out in winter; I feared that racist folks would attack us and we'd be all alone.

Perhaps the fears were unfounded but they were nevertheless there. In Spring 2020, while the world was in a pandemic lockdown, we stumble upon a listing for an in-town Colonial Revival with hardwood floors, an interesting history, and a lush garden looking out to a forest of tall, sturdy trees. Though it no longer had a mountain view (the trees and the neighbor's house took care of that), it had enough to enchant us, good ch'i included. And we'd have neighbors.

Neighbors who'd welcome us with flowers, fruits, gardening tools, plants, and pumpkins. Who'd share their homemade jams. Who'd water our plants and shovel snow off our driveway while we were away. Who had "Hate Has No Home Here" signs on their front lawn. Considering that Pennsylvania would have the highest level of white supremacist propaganda in 2021, I take these as wins.

Throwing my painfully thought-out house plans aside, we decide to buy this home and deepen our Pennsylvania roots.

On our first spring, though a germaphobe, I cup the earth with my bare hands; my fingers caress the rich, riverine soil. I add leaf compost onto the planting bed, surprised I'm playing with dirt. This is where my tomatoes and basil will grow, where dahlias will explode with flowers year after year.

On this land where branches arch and spread like dancers' arms, I study light, dappled light, and shade, noting their movements through the seasons when trees are robed in green or ring rust-gold, haunt in sepia or bewitch in white, break into buds or lapse into leaves.

These woods are now my mountains; my music takes on their curves and hues. They woo like lovers and watch like sentinels. I whisper thanks.

* * *

Dave and I renew our vows in front of the Japanese maple as summer greens morph into scarlet. Our neighbor officiates. We celebrate not just our love but that of our friends with whom we spent the pandemic: Zoom happy hours, outdoor gatherings even in winter, the social-distanced indoor Thanksgiving dinner with windows open and the heat cranked up. The woods watch and wonder. Again, we say I do.

We haven't kayaked much in the two years since we moved. But we go back to the river like pilgrims of the seasons and admire the ways the mountains and trees rise from their other selves. Is this double-vision like the Tagalog's twin souls: one tied to the body, the other free and unbound? Or is it one self that's mirrored, magnified, or split?

Perhaps we, too, are the river. Inside us are fragments of a braided past—land, language, heritage, home—and we wash them away, fossils found further downstream, minerals deposited onto some forgotten terrace.

The river inside: ever-ancient, ever-new. It will move and carve, sculpt and split, it will gather and let go. It will cut and it will double. It will bring me the sky in a dream. It will be forded to reach another shore.

I will flow along.

Pennsylvania: the basin that holds both worlds—perhaps all my worlds. Sky and river as one, rocked and cradled by the earth, the mountains touching all. Mountain, river, earth, and sky: the dwellings of sacred spirits, according to my ancestors, they, too, are my Pennsylvania elements. Irreducible, primary, primal.

Let the river wash me away. Let the forest swallow my remains. Let the ocean not let me rest.

AURORA BONNER

Fractures

Woodbourne is tranquil today, with a sky of pure ultramarine and cumulous clouds so thick they might burst. Fall has not yet set in, the daytime air is still hot, but the cool nights are beginning to soften the grasses to chartreuse and reveal glimpses of crimson, orange, and gold among the greenery. Mallards maneuver through the dozens of tree carcasses that cut through the bog like broken signposts. Red-winged blackbirds trill me a warning as I stand on the dock near their homes in the cattails.

Woodbourne Forest and Wildlife Preserve, the Nature Conservatory's first preserve in Pennsylvania, offers a reprieve while visiting my in-laws, who live just a few miles south of here. According to The Nature Conservatory, Woodbourne contains one of the largest areas of old-growth forest in northeast Pennsylvania but is being threatened by invasive species like the hemlock wooly adelgid and emerald ash borer, and by overgrazing deer. I wonder how long Hemlock Loop will remain, and why their website doesn't list "fracking" as a threat, or "gas companies" as invasive species.

There are some days when I look at rural Pennsylvania and question my desire to leave these woods. I've lived in their forests all of my life, and on most days I'm still marveled at the endless mountains and wellspring of nature. Pennsylvania feels like a jungle, the humidity so dense in the summer it gathers on my eyelashes in droplets during my morning runs. Vegetation erupts in crevices, ivies reaching through the cracks of my wooden deck, maples sprouting in the burls of the red oak that towers over my house, violets pushing through the mulch of my vegetable garden.

It takes almost no effort to grow here—if you're a plant. The Amish Deer Tongue lettuce seeds sown in the spring will reseed and sprout in the fall whether collected meticulously with tweezers as sun rolls out for high summer, or whether they fall in the heat. Garlic-mustard weed, bristled knotweed, and other invasive plants germinate faster than the million pounds of herbicides sprayed each year can strangle them out. But to grow as a human here in rural Pennsylvania takes considerably more effort.

Rural Pennsylvania is littered with small towns and rural cities—once booming areas known for lumber or coal that have declined through decades of progress, leaving abandoned buildings, empty storefronts, high unemployment rates, high poverty rates, innumerable mental health issues, and Trump signs that just won't go away. To love rural America is to be enamored with its palette of mountains, creeks, and wildflowers but confined by its beliefs, politics, and adversity. The lack of opportunities is stifling.

My parents and their friends moved to Bradford County, Pennsylvania, in the 1970s to live a communal life. They were all looking for the same thing—to live a life surrounded by nature and to push back against the injustices of "the man." I was born in a hand-built cabin with no running water, with enough woods to keep us kids happy and an apple orchard up the dirt road. When the apple farmers sprayed their fields we became captives in our little cabin, our parents standing guard. After some time, what felt like weeks, we'd be allowed back outside, with the false impression we were safe from the toxic chemicals, as if the paraquat and glyphosate that Monsanto and Chevron were selling to gunslinging weed-haters everywhere would not stay for a lifetime in the soil. My parents eventually left the cabin to look for job opportunities. Their dream of living off the land, as big and as full as it was, could not pay the bills.

When the gas surge first began, homeowners in the Endless Mountains and Pennsylvania Wilds, areas that are now more known for the Marcellus Shale boom than for their natural beauty, trembled with anticipation. The rumor of jobs and money rode in with the frackers, a promise so full of possibility that it didn't really matter whether it was true. In areas riddled with debt and unemployment, sandwiched between crime and opioid addiction, a broken promise may be the only type of promise we know. Besides, isn't a broken promise better than no promise at all?

Some Pennsylvania residents signed contracts the very first time a gas representative showed up at their homes, only to hear their neighbors were offered twice as much the second go-around. The warier residents conducted neighborhood roundtables to educate themselves on what these offers really meant with information provided by the gas representatives. They, too, signed. Some held out until their plots were the only ones left unsigned, a blotch of red on their gas maps. By the time they realized their holdout didn't matter, that the frackers could simply drill around them whether they signed or not, some capitulated. By then, the sign-on bonuses were no longer offered. Today, gas wells surround my childhood home in Bradford County, which has more gas wells than almost any other county in Pennsylvania.

My son was born the day after we purchased our second home, outside of the beautiful town of Tunkhannock, further up the Susquehanna River and across from the Endless Mountains Nature Center's land and trails. We chose our home because it had a plot big enough for a large garden and enough woods for our children to run wild. And it did not have a gas contract, something we saw as a huge perk. Pregnancy had filled me with joy, and the excitement of living off the land, raising my children as I'd been raised, felt right.

Three days after we'd signed our home contract, a gas well malfunctioned and sprayed thousands of gallons of fracking fluid into the earth, only one mile from our property. I was in the hospital with my baby boy, but others in our township were cautioned to vacate the premises. Because there was no explosion, Carrizo Gas & Oil quickly announced that all was safe. Immediate testing showed there was nothing wrong with the air and water, or with continuing to rape the land. When we approached Carrizo about our concerns, they laughed, but offered us royalties.

The trailhead to Woodbourne is right next to Route 29, the road that cuts through most of the eastern region of the state, but the parking lot is easy to miss. Now, I know to look for the new Cabot building and the Gassearch Drilling Corporation sign. The trailhead's right past them. On the right. The trail descends to a bog where quiet contemplation can reward you with sightings of winter wrens, beaver, pileated woodpeckers, red-tailed hawks, the songs of warblers, or the coo of barred owls. It's easy to forget that fracking liquid is being pumped down wells spearing through dirt and groundwater on every side of its boundaries.

Soon after a gas explosion in Dimock, the town closest to Woodbourne Preserve, the state claimed they wanted to rethink gas drilling regulations. Despite what they said, the Environmental Defense Fund still found that methane emissions appeared to be five times higher than what has been reported by the drilling companies years after that explosion. I wonder if I lit a match, the water in the bog at Woodbourne would ignite like the drinking water did for the Dimock residents down the road.

After the incident in 2009, there was some publicity around the gas problems in Pennsylvania. The 2010 documentary *Gasland*, featured Dimock and the thirteen water wells that were contaminated with methane there, including the one that exploded. Arsenic, barium, DEHP, glycol compounds, manganese, phenol, and sodium levels were said to exceed safety levels. In 2010, *Vanity Fair Magazine* referred to the issues in Dimock and other Pennsylvania towns as "A Colossal Fracking Mess." Lawsuits ensued and though the gas company responsible for the well was ordered to provide residents with clean water and to stop drilling, that only lasted until 2011—about a year later. By 2015, all but two families of the forty original had withdrawn their lawsuits. The two who continued were awarded 4 million dollars by a jury. Finally, after years of fighting, a victory against gas, or so it seemed.

But that supposed victory only lasted a year, too, when a federal judge, Martin C. Carlson, sided with Cabot, saying that the jury's verdict "must be vacated." By now, the stir around the cases in Dimock has died off, and they continue to drill for gas. There have been over 225 drilling violations in Dimock alone. How long would a group of people have to hold out in order to fight the politics of money? How long can we continue to fight from a place of decency against a place of power? How long until all decency is gone?

We sold our home in Tunkhannock and moved away from gas country. But I can't get its natural beauty out of my heart. On the Woodburn trail, halfway around Woodruff Hill Trail, where it overlaps with Copes Ramble Trail, there's a creek that cuts between the two. The emerald pools are cool to touch, so I unlaced my hiking boots and peeled my socks off to take a soak. The air is heavy and wet here, cooler than the rest of the hike. It felt good, but after running through my water bottle, I was still thirsty, that unquenchable thirst that comes on days when heat and humidity fight neck and neck with each other. The water in the creek was so clear that even where it pooled you could see the smooth rock below. I imagined gulping it down, sucking big handfuls in through cupped fists. But what we see is not what is in this water. You can't wash the paraquat away, no matter how many times you rinse it. It's in the dirt, it's in the water. Progress is slow, they say. But what they mean is, we can't make money off honoring the land.

Frantz Hill

The road up Frantz Hill is well shaded, and fragrant with phlox (or what we think is phlox), and a kind of brush whose blossoms offer a sweet honeysuckle scent. Frantz Hill isn't tall, but at one thousand feet, it's easily the highest point near town. At the crest of the hill, everything opens into meadow land.

A church has been up on the hilltop for a very long time, at least judging from the tombstones in the church yard, the oldest of which mark graves from people born in the early 1800s. The present church is a fairly modern structure with a ridged metal roof. It humbly squats on the ridge line overlooking two nice vistas. The one to the east offers a good view of the innumerable wrinkles and folds that make up some of the foothills of the Alleghenies, but it would be impossible to see them through the stained glass. Looking west, one sees the ridge of Bald Eagle Mountain, but not the West Branch of the Susquehanna that snakes along its base. Looking south one sees Hughesville, a mile away nestled in a corner of the flat narrow valley bottom.

We'd come up to the top of this hill mostly at night, during the odd full moon, and on a few occasions when the comet Kahoutek was visible. As comets go, Kahoutek was something of a letdown, with its dim and dusty limping across the sky. The moonlight on the rolling hills, on the other hand, was invariably a fine sight.

I'm not entirely sure why the cemetery sits on this site. Around here, one often finds cemeteries planted on spots with a good view. This is antithetical to the views of the wise Renaissance physician Marsilio Ficino, who urged people to consider sites such as this, airy, high, and suns splashed, as an ideal place for a home.

The dead, so far as I know, do not clamor for fresh air, but they get plenty of it up here. Later, it occurred to me that driving a well on the hill might have been a problem, and exchanging a nice view for more readily available fresh water supplies might have been a good deal.

Rhenna likes to poke around old tombstones. As noted, there are quite a few up there, some crude slabs of field stone, engraved at home by the family. Examining some of the dates on the stones, you can readily deduce that, even though ignoring Ficino's advice about the healthy properties of building on the top of a hill, even those who lived down in the hollows around Frantz Hill tended to live a long time. There are a surprising number of people who made it into their seventies, and a handful of those who lived to ninety or so. This is offset by the sad sight of those who failed to make it past a year, some lamentably checking out after a single day. In the oldest section of the churchyard, these extremes seemed to hold sway—it seems one was either an old timer or a very brief memory.

The lilacs behind the church are still in full bloom, in contrast to the ones at home, one thousand feet below, which are now faded and frowsy. The air is soft and welcome as a kiss on the brow, the sun neither blistering nor begrudging.

A pair of red-winged blackbirds dart from the lilacs to the field and back again. Their crimson markings are brilliant in this light. Not straying far from the lilac bush, another bird sits preening itself and singing, now and again fluttering up and showing off the bright white bars on his wings. Without these bands, he's otherwise a small dun bird, but the display is impressive, and he knows it. On the strength of this, he sets out to bully a much larger robin from feeding not far away. The robin isn't finding anything he wants, but he's full of himself at the moment, and for now, brio display is working for him. The robin flies a good twenty feet away and watches, but each attempt he makes to get back to his former feeding ground is met with the vireo's aggressive fluttering.

A few barn swallows dart in and out of the churchyard, swooping down and snacking on a few darting insects I can barely make out, thus shortening their already brief life span.

Some other people are up here as well, tending the new graves at either end of the churchyard. They don't seem to be watching the acrobatics of the swallows, nor the showy procession of the red-winged blackbirds, and not even the noisy preening and defensive gestures of the blue-headed vireo against the much larger robin distract them from their work. If they notice anything, they probably wonder why I am watching birds up here.

It's still and quiet enough that I can hear the metal on the roof expand and contract according to how the sunlight settles on it. The tiny flowers of faux strawberries litter the grass, providing a splendid adornment for otherwise unattended markers of folks long since gone by, their own kin perhaps also having died off or moved far away.

It's difficult to figure out our funereal customs, perhaps as troubling as sorting out how we deal with one another while still alive. I've never much cared for the idea of burial as such, but given the choice, a long eternity of afternoons on Frantz Hill doesn't seem such a bad possibility. However it happens, I'd like the remnants of my bones to make their creaking way into something once again alive; something one of those birds would snatch into their bills and make good use of, flying back to their nests and sing, pleased with their find.

GRANT CLAUSER

In the Boughs of Trees

It was one of those in-between days in Pennsylvania, temperature in the low 50s when if you didn't know the date, the gray sky, bare trees, and rain's-gonna-come feeling could pass for anything from November to March. I was puttering around in some woods between housing developments, a small ravine that was technically township parkland in name only but was too steep and rocky to be useful. It was a favorite place to let my hound dog chase whatever scents would send him into a frenzy of delighted grunts and tail wags, but for some reason, until today, I'd never bothered to look up.

Around fifteen feet above my shoulders was the unmistakable ramshackle remains of an old treefort perched in the branches of a walnut tree. Not a hunter's deer stand, though I see those frequently enough. This bore the shoddy, but optimistic workmanship of kids—mismatched boards now faded to moth gray, nails in Richter scale alignment, and a rope swing, though probably used for hauling up snacks as there was no pond or creek to swing over. I knew all the signs because many decades ago I too was a bush league carpenter of forts.

My first one wasn't much more than a platform supported by branches of a single tree. My father built it for my brother and me in our backyard in the 1970s. I remember it being fifty feet in the air, exhilarating in its danger. My father says it was more like twelve feet, a more reasonable height corroborated by my brother, but I'll stick with my side of the story. It got us high enough to look down at the neighbor's horses, and I'd spend hours up there with a stack of comic books, imagining this place was my secret superhero hideout.

I grew up (and still live) in what I call rural-adjacent parts of Pennsylvania. I could walk from my house to cornfields, creeks and patches of woods. But the neighborhood felt suburban (I could also ride my bike to the mall's video arcade). Despite my proximity to halogen streetlights and 7-Elevens, my time in treeforts still made childhood feel a bit wild, something unfortunately my own children never experienced.

The first one I actually built, with help from my friend Kevin, was in the woods just behind our house in Palmer Township. Through the fence gate, up the path, and I was in oak and hickory woods full of red-backed salamanders, club moss, and the occasional ring-necked pheasant. I like to think I pioneered the design of this treefort. It had three sides cornered by sturdy trees, long 2x4s connected them together, and then a floor laid over the 2x4s. The hut had two stories, walled by whatever plywood I and my friends could sneak out of parents' garages or salvage from some older kid's abandoned forts. Inside we lined it with carpet scraps, and decorated it with posters torn from *Circus* or *Fangoria* magazines.

There was a definite culture to treeforts back then. Each patch of woods seemed to have one, and you better know whose fort it was before you tried anything around there. Perhaps American colonialism had trickled down into our tween brains, but building a fort felt like staking a claim, one that had to be defended. Most woods' treeforts weren't the parent-approved clubhouses you see on TV. A woods treehouse couldn't be in a yard. Preferably the land ownership had to be somewhat ambiguous—just out in the woods, as we knew them. Someone owned the land, but we usually didn't know or care who—there's that colonial mindset again.

We budding architects and Daniel Boones practiced a kind of fuck-around-and-find-out attitude to construction. If a board wasn't quite long enough, nail another board onto it. If a board looked a little weak or rotten, nail another board onto it. If you could jump on it once without collapse, it would last a lifetime. Concepts like load-bearing and span limits meant nothing to us, but somehow we kept the walls and floors up with luck and a bucket of ten-penny nails.

Raids were a constant threat. They were also the best way to get more wood to expand or reinforce your fort. I'd spend a lot of summer nights in my cramped garrison acting as sentry, eating potato chips and reading comics by flashlight. Every noise out in the dry leaves could be a rival, though more likely it was a deer or skunk. One morning, after a night spent in my bed rather than the fort, I walked up the trail to see all the walls missing (along with my RadioShack radio).

Most of the woodlands back then were more or less connected by a network of trails worn down by a combination of pot smokers and dirtbikers. Kevin and I found the missing walls when we were riding our BMX bikes from one hollow to another. There they were, fastened to someone else's treefort. Unfortunately, we were in Billy Marshall's territory now, and he was older, bigger, and a little scary, which essentially meant the end of our fort.

The most impressive treefort I witnessed as a kid was built on the edge of Hackett's Park. I always assumed it was haunted because not fifty yards away were the foundations of a stone house and well, crumbled into ruins at least a century before, or at least it seemed that way to me then. This was a four by four: four walls and four floors, each story accessed by its own hatch door. The first floor was only about shoulder height off the ground, and each ceiling low enough to make a fourteen-year-old boy crouch, but it had a few windows (a luxury in treeforts) covered by clear plastic sheeting. Spray-painted cusses and "keep out" warnings adorned the sides, while a string of beer cans around the perimeter served as an alarm system. Despite its tower-of-strength appearance, a park demolition crew reduced it to scrap a few weeks after it went up.

A couple years later we became the older, scarier, kids, and when we built our three-story McMansion, pitched on a hillside so one wall was only about four feet off the ground, the back wall was thirty-feet high. We salvaged and raided enough wood, some of it dangerously rotten, to build a structure that could hold about eight kids, as long as you didn't mind rubbing shoulders. Somewhere we got a hold of a few large rolls of tar paper and used that to cover the roof against rain. We managed to squeeze two fold-up futons through the small trap door, so we had something to recline on. In a supreme act of stupidity, we decided to make this an all-season treefort by building in a fireplace constructed from a rusty hibachi, some sheet metal, and a stovepipe we found in a trash heap in another part of the woods. Remarkably, we never burned the place down, due in part to how damp the whole thing was most of the time.

Weather and wildlife presented as much a threat to treefort longevity as raids. Untreated wood rots, nails rust, and storms took out whole trees and whatever was attached to them. I abandoned one fort, a pit style with a plywood ceiling and floor, when a racoon moved in. If you stayed away from your fort for more than a week in the summer, you had to be mindful of wasp nests. Sometimes it was hard to tell if the creaking and scratching sounds were one of our support beams about to give up, or an animal chewing through. Both bad news.

While treeforts were mostly an early teens game, we continued to maintain our McMansion, adding supports or repairing the tar paper, well into our high school years, mostly because it served as a reasonably safe place to drink or smoke weed. Occasionally we'd talk dates into the fort, but usually, they'd take one look at that sagging shack nailed to the trees and decide they wanted nothing to do with that horror show.

Kevin had given me the news over the phone, so on a break my freshman year at college, I went back to our woods to see for myself. Someone, probably the landowner, had completely demolished the fort and even carried off the wood. The only evidence it had ever been there were some bent nails in the trees and a new "posted" sign. I lit a cigarette in toast to what had been, then walked out.

* * *

I may be overgeneralizing, but the try-first/ask-questions-later approach to youth in the 1970s and 80s seems to have ended by the time grunge music arrived. It probably has more to do with the parents, like me, wondering how the hell we survived our own stupidity, than anything particular about our kids' generation. When we weren't occupied with our forts, we were jumping our BMX bikes over pit fires or playing war with BB guns. Our parents didn't much ask what we were doing in the woods, as long as we came home in time for dinner. My own kids' formative years included supervised playdates, organized group activities, and considerably less danger. I still don't know who had it better.

What I do know is when I found another old treefort a few weeks ago, I climbed. The boards making the ladder up the tree wobbled and shifted, and one broke free of its nails under my boot, but I shuffled up to the platform anyway. Lucky for me, the base was supported by a couple of good beams thick as fence posts, and I kept my weight positioned over those. The plywood floor didn't look like it could support a bird after a good meal. Because the roof was half collapsed, I had plenty of light to look around the small room. There were some old soda cans, a sleeping bag chewed up by squirrels, and a pile of leaves that may have been the squirrel's nest. I couldn't help thinking about the kid or kids who built this, living their adventure, getting their first taste of independence like little homesteaders.

The US Department of Agriculture says there are about 16 billion trees in Pennsylvania, many of them in the forests that cover sixty percent of the state, but also in backyards, hidden gullies, and abandoned lots. That's a lot of trees, and to me, that's also a lot of opportunity. Now in my fifities, climbing trees is less wise than it was when I was forty years lighter, and even then I did a lot of unwise things in trees. But I've always believed that a little recklessness is necessary for wisdom. Hanging from a branch with a hammer, a couple of nails in my mouth, wasn't so much about making a fort as it was daring anyone or anything to stop me from doing it. Perhaps weather, age, and industry eventually catch up with every kid's treefort (and every kid), but that sense of doing something risky, having done something, lasts a lifetime.

BILL CONLOGUE

Driving

When I lived on the farm, I drove cars, trucks, and tractors, but I didn't think much about it. My brother Jack loved to drive, whether a car or a truck, and my father and brother Danny could spend hours on a tractor, cutting, raking, or baling hay. That I was less enthused may have been due, as I look back, to my relationship to the farm. From the time I was a child, fear haunted me that it would be lost. I felt pulses of anxiety, from low-level embarrassment to something approaching terror. But these feelings—so everyday, and yet so defining—were so unremarkable that I didn't know what they meant then, and I'm not sure that I do now.

In my senior year of high school, a state trooper stopped me for speeding on Stillwater stretch, the two miles of Route 171 that parallel the reservoir. Bit players in *The Grand Tour*, two classmates and I were late for practice. I was doing, maybe, seventy. . . . The officer didn't careen after us, flashing lights and blaring sirens, running us to a roadblock where cops stood with guns drawn, which I'd seen in movies and on TV. No, as we approached the dam, he stepped into view and crooked a finger at us. I hit the brakes, pulled over, and stopped, dreading the grief my haste might bring. I cut the engine and waited . . .

May, 1971, 7:30 P.M.: a Chrysler hurtles south past the stop sign at Belmont Corners, striking a pea green Biscayne moving west. Both shoot across the road, hammering into a car parked at Steve's Bar. The Chrysler driver passes out, his passenger screams, and my brother Bobby falls, dazed, from the Biscayne. Steve's owner appears, shouting about cops and his car, and not long later my brother Jack, underage and eastbound for a Cochecton roadhouse, pulls over to inspect the wrecks. He turns to Bobby to say the obvious: the Biscayne is totaled. He then takes its

8-track, climbs into his own car, and takes off. Coming to me as family lore, the story made the intersection meaningful. Speed and violence mark the spot, so whenever I drive through there, I remember that anything can happen, at any time, so I slow down, read the signs, and glance both ways.

The workhorse on the place, the tractor was two years older than me, and was one of the first diesels that John Deere marketed, in 1961, a time before rollover bars. A tricycle design, with power steering and power brakes, the 3010 pulled and powered the haybine, baler, and corn chopper, and it tugged plows, disks, and wagons. For snowstorms, we attached a bucket loader to the front to clear the driveway, a steep thousand yards, and when the milk tanker got stuck in drifts, we used chains and the 3010 to pull it out and on up to milk house.

In winter, hauling manure was a daily chore. We had a New Idea manure spreader, which we kept hooked to the tractor. On cold days, a heavy-duty extension cord powered a heater to get the engine to turn over. No one knew how many hours were on it, the counter had long stopped working, and by the 1990s, the diesel looked its age: dented hood, wired-together side panels, only ghosts of green paint. And it sometimes refused to start. So we parked it in the driveway, near the barn. If it didn't roar to life, we rolled it to catch it in gear.

One March—a day of snow flurries, mud, and cold—I climbed aboard the 3010 and turned the key. Nothing. I took it out of park, let it roll, and popped the clutch. No sound. It kept rolling, the manure spreader pushing. The second try: no. Here the driveway turned ninety degrees left, away from the house, and ran level for a few hundred feet before plunging to the road below. The wheel took some effort to steer. The third try: no.

Popped out of gear, the tractor picked up speed, the manure spreader rattling behind, the pitch drawing us down faster and faster. The driveway teed to a dirt road, barbed wire fences on both sides, Bobby's house a hundred feet farther on. Bouncing in the seat, I could only think, make the turn, make the turn.

Braced to steer, I pulled. The front wheels slid, slowed, jackknifing tractor and spreader, tossing me off to land spread-eagled on a fence, just in time to watch the tractor's back wheel roll toward me, coming within inches of my face before falling back . . .

Jack unloaded rigs for Roadway at the Tannersville hub before landing his first truck driving job: hauling dead car batteries to a lead-recovery plant in Throop. Acid ate the trailers, and he often came home with holes in his clothes. The place is now a Superfund site.

Later a long-hauler for American Pipe and Plastics, he drove his pickup about forty-five minutes to Kirkwood, New York, to reach his tractor-trailer; from there he made deliveries up and down the East Coast, and as far west as the Mississippi.

A farm-bound fourteen-year-old, I thought how great it would be to see what he saw. I had never been more than a few hours from home before he invited me to ride with him to Rhode Island. We traveled overnight. I vaguely recall waking as we approached a toll booth, sensing the stop, hearing voices. The sun rising as we arrived in Providence, he pulled into a construction site, parked, and promptly fell asleep.

Rested, I found myself at loose ends, so I climbed from the cab and walked around the rig, kicking tires, checking this and that, my red-white-and-blue company cap pulled low. When three construction workers stopped to chat, I kept nodding, clueless because I couldn't understand their New England accents. We spoke the same language, but I couldn't process a word they said. Puzzled and amused, they drifted away. It would be a long while before I visited there again, or ventured north of Boston.

Long-haul trucking kept Jack away for long stretches, so he looked for work that would bring him home each day. After American Pipe and Plastics, he settled into delivering liquor to state-run liquor stores for Kane is Able, compiling a near-perfect safety record.

We had a work truck on the farm, nothing fancy, a 1966 Chevy three-quarter-ton, red trimmed in white, with removable racks. My father hauled heifers, feed, and sawdust with it, and tossed in the back rolls of barbed wire, sledgehammers, and locust posts. My mother drove it to the Tastee-Freeze, the post office, and the grocery store, and to churches, the neighbors', and firemen's picnics. It introduced me to helplessness.

Crammed in the cab of the truck, we were hauling home a load of anthracite from Dreeter's, the coal dealer in Childs. Stuck in the middle, a six-year-old, I had to move my legs every time my father shifted gears as the Chevy labored up hills and around bends. A teenager, Jack rode shotgun. As we started down the long, east-facing hill in Griswold's Gap, the brakes gave out. The truck picked up speed. My father tried downshifting, gears grinding. Jack smoked while I stared, wide-eyed, at a blind curve drawing closer. We swung wide, wheels lifting, the truck tilting then righting itself. The road straightened, stretching toward the Belmont-Easton Turnpike. The truck flew through the T-intersection, shot across a yard, and swung hard left, fanning coal, bounced in and out of a ditch, and landed hard on a gravel drive. Facing west, we rolled to a stop in the right-of-way of Tennessee Gas. From there, we rode home, in low gear, up and over hills, my heart pumping in low-grade alarm.

Our dairy farm was in the New York City milkshed. For almost eight years, from 1964 until 1972, my father hauled milk to Herrick Center, to a processing plant beside the O&W tracks. I sometimes went with him, anxious to help. Six or seven years old, I'd watch him load our ten or so galvanized steel cans, which were not light, about 110 pounds full, and then we'd climb into the truck to visit three farms, one five or so miles away. As he loaded their cans, he exchanged a few words with each farmer, who usually had a bit of news, or maybe a complaint about our lateness. The Chevy had high racks, so my father could stack cans, which he secured with chains, with me hooking one end, or getting brushed aside.

Rolling through Belmont Corners, we moved milk from the Lackawaxen to the Lackawanna watershed; from there, a rail car carried it across the Delaware to the Hudson watershed. Other farmers often arrived at the processing plant before us, so we sometimes had to wait in line for a turn at the dock, maybe ten minutes. Unloading meant placing each can onto a line of rollers that disappeared inside. A second set of rollers returned the empties, clean, wet, and warm. My father transferred them to the truck; more hindrance than help, I'd roll one to the front. A red number painted on each identified the farm that owned it. Before heading home, we revisited the farms. All this happened each morning, every morning, after milking and before 10:00. My father then turned to the day's other chores.

When the plant in Herrick Center closed, my father drove the truck eight miles more, north to the Lakewood plant, also on the O&W line. When Lakewood shuttered, he headed to Honesdale, ten miles in the other direction, until he had to decide between driving to Nicholson or installing a bulk tank. Nearly thirty miles off, Nicholson was a long drive for our ten, sometimes twenty, cans, but a bulk tank was expensive and came with a haulage fee so that a dual axle would come to drain it. The message was clear: cans—and small farms—were on the way out. I felt the danger: My father had to choose whether to enlarge the herd or quit. To house more cows, he built an addition on the barn. In the next ten years, the dual axle became a tri axle and then a tractor-trailer, which demanded a new driveway and room to turn around . . .

In its last days on the farm, the truck sat in the field above the barn, all but lost in high grass. When it disappeared, I knew only that someone had towed it away, likely for parts. No new truck replaced it, and when I saw it again, I didn't recognize it. With the racks gone, it looked more beaten than I remembered, and I found it totally out of context.

The summer after I finished high school, I worked in Simpson, just north of Carbondale, at Doyle & Roth, a fabricator of heat exchangers. The factory sits on land that the Delaware & Hudson Canal Company bought in 1825, two weeks after crews began digging the ditch that carried coal to the Hudson River. In 1906 and 1909, the company sold pieces of the property, which adjoins the Jefferson branch of the Erie Railroad, to American Welding Company, a maker of flues, furnaces, and boilers. American Welding sold the land in 1945; Doyle & Roth occupied the plant in 1947. My brother Bobby spent most of his work life there as a pipe fitter. He hated it. He loved the farm.[1]

At Doyle & Roth, I did odd jobs: fetching tools, sweeping floors, moving bundles of pipe. Sometimes, though, I ground metal, mainly smoothing burrs and edges on small shells. When a ten-foot one didn't quite accommodate a collection of pipes and baffles, I had the job of sledgehammering the outside and grinding the inside, which meant sparks shooting up the arc until they reached the top, only to fall on my exposed neck. Every so often, the foreman would stop me, climb inside, and rotate a steel stick. Only after scores of false tries did the rod move freely. The work paid just above minimum wage, and I had to be worthy of my hire, which Bobby had arranged.

1. "The plant . . . American Welding Company": Walster Corporation, 154-155; "a manufacturer . . . boilers": "Welding Co."; "American . . . 1945": "Purchasers"; "Doyle . . . 1947": "Strike-Bound."

One day, the foreman directed me and another summer worker to haul inside dozens of pipes that fitters would cut and weld and bundle. All of it we piled onto a sad-looking truck. As I climbed in, the cab felt familiar. I put the thing in drive, but the contraption barely had strength to move. With my fellow worker atop the pipe to hold the pile in place, I inched the truck slowly toward the door. The foreman approached, shaking his head, muttering at our stupidity. After ordering us to set the pipe to one side—and as he walked away, shouting that three trips would have been smarter than one—I heard my father and knew the truck.

The truck had a good run, Jack followed his dream of driving, and my father lived to see the farm passed on. Bobby straddled two lives, working at Doyle & Roth during the day and bearing the burden of the farm at night and on weekends, but I couldn't do the same, and the farm passed from the family. We did what we could to keep it, I suppose, but it wasn't enough, not near enough.

TODD DAVIS

What the Old Ones Show Us

A storm rumbled through last night, flickering dark windows like a child playing with a flashlight beneath a bedsheet. This morning the air cleared, and temperatures plummeted nearly twenty degrees. We haven't fished for some time. Low summer flows and work to be done in the garden. But today the stream looks like the month of May. It's good to feel the cold water swirling around our legs, to lean against the current and imagine a pocket beneath the surface where a fish waits, watching for the drift of a caddis, ready to charge and engulf temptation.

Noah moves ahead of me in the streambed, walking through a green tunnel, the rest of the world walled off. In July, the woods are thick with leaves, and the rhododendron that crave water grow in dense screens along the creeks that carve the hollows of the Allegheny Front. Here old water has descended over hundreds of thousands of years, the passage of time marked by what erodes, geologic presence trickling into humid absence.

Water claps stone, obscuring the splash of our steps. Ahead of us a great blue heron wades. The rhododendron boughs hide us from her as we cling to the tunnel's edges. The bird's slate-colored wings are nearly as wide as the stream. We watch her stillness, admire her predatory patience. I can't help but imagine the history written between the feathered folds. More precisely, the prehistoric divinity hidden in these intricate patterns. A predatory angel born of another time, she appears to carry the weight of millennia lightly, a joyous concert of evolution playing along her limbs. Perhaps she's aware of us, willing to allow us to come into her presence. More likely she's simply unwilling to let us ruin the fishing. We're here for the same reason.

I want the trout to divulge themselves, to tell me something of their lives, something of the stream and how it undulates beneath the surface of things. Most of the time they're hidden, eating what emerges from beneath stone. Unless they're coaxed to the surface, they'll sidle beside a rock, stay where the current storms overhead but is barely perceptible below, a pocket of safety and rest.

Today with the water high but falling, brook trout grow bold, unafraid of the heron that stalks ahead of us, the kingfisher that click-clacks the air, racing the strip of sky the stream prunes from the woods. Some of that fearlessness is foolhardy. We've already seen one kingfisher with a fish draped across the half-open door of its beak. But some of that fearlessness makes sense. There's more water to escape into, more depth for eye and talon to navigate through.

Every time a fly touches the water, a take follows. Floats are short and the eruption from beneath the surface breathtaking, a gasp at the grace of a body emerging in an eyeblink, a slant or perpendicular thrust, then a curving back, a disappearance, making me ask if I've truly witnessed what I think I have.

It doesn't matter how many times I spy a trout rise, I'm still awed. Enchanted and spellbound and, yes, addicted. Each rise leaves me unfulfilled, the concentric ripples moving away into a resolution of nothingness.

Most of the fish in these headwaters are six inches, a few reach eight or nine. Beauty rests not in the size of the bodies but in their design, the glowing orange coals along male bellies, the purple coloration that engulfs female sides, the spectacle of olive vermiculation atop their backs. To hold a speckled trout is to grasp stained glass as it turns to muscle, a fluid prism that bends light and color with a strength that belies size.

Noah and I have already fished a few hours, covering more than a mile of stream in a seam that runs north to south, turning after a time to the east to join the big river in the valley. We still have miles to cover before this water turns too small and the fish vanish.

I'm not sure how much farther to go. There's the question whether more fishing might spoil the day. Already gifted so many strikes. The strong tug that pulls the mind under water. The persistent reeling in, holding a glistening body, examining the scar on a side where the teeth of a larger fish or the claw of some ravenous bird raked months or years before. And while on some days we do eat these fish—delivering the quivering pink flesh to a darkened pan, butter melting across its surface and onto our tongues—today it feels good to open the hand to mercy, to see how mercy swims away to hide itself in the stream again.

More than half a century of walking makes me think we should head home, knees aching a bit. But I look to the sky, through the kaleidoscopic canopy and on to the everlasting blue. Shafts of sunlight descend haphazardly. I simply can't waste an hour of this perfect day.

With the decision made, we head upstream toward the boulder pool where the water makes a moderate turn and the land slides against an enormous rock that's broad as a shack. The eddy created on the left, downward side is deep and expands to the edge of the current that rushes from above. Trout can hold along the quickening water and still experience a degree of tranquility. An ancient hemlock provides shade. This deep in the hollow the ridges rise directly from the streambed at a precipitous incline. It's that topographical difficulty that spared these old trees.

There are all kinds of words for momentous events, singularities, and anomalies, like "hundred-year-flood," "storm-of-the-century," "fish-of-a-lifetime." We try to name the extraordinary and often fail. But in the attempt we're reminded nothing exists outside of this world, no matter how mystifying, mysterious, or miraculous. The very nature of existence is staggering enough.

The question is how simply to be present, to accept the moment for what it reveals. Not to let the mind hurry ahead to the stories that will be told, to the implication that what has passed will likely never happen again.

And so when the brook trout assails the fly I've drifted, rising vertically from the bottom of the pool, turning on it and driving down in the exact same direction it has come, back to the bottom, I'm not prepared for the next few minutes and how they will change the way I see this stream, the way I perceive the life of a fish and its connection to mine.

My rod bends toward the point of breaking. The line runs fast, then stops. I pull back. The line creeps forward. Inches incrementally toward the boulder. Then nothing. A heaviness. No movement at all. Yet I can't retrieve the line.

I shout to Noah that I think the trout's wrapped me around a sunken log. A ponderous anxiety fixes to the ribcage, a feeling anglers know too well when they're sure a special fish has alluded them, breaking the line, tangling them, and spitting a fly.

I move forward into the pool, water rising around me. I bring the rod tip toward me and grasp the line to tug a bit harder, hoping to release the snag without breaking off the fly.

The slightest vibration works against my fingers. Can I hope the fish is still on? No, it's simply the current. Then another vibration, clearly a shake. I bring the rod handle back to my grip, pull a bit, and the fish is swimming again, out from under that ancient boulder, swimming toward me fast and down past, then back by. All while I seek to maintain some tension.

Noah grabs the net from my back as I try my best to guide the fish toward him. The two of us together land a brook trout fully fifteen inches in length. A female with a slick purple luster, a jaw gray with age, teeth that have devoured fry and fingerlings. She's so much bigger than any fish we imagined could swim in this small water.

Brook trout can live five or six years, but it's rare in the wild. The attrition from fry to mature fish is significant. Once mature, the likelihood of even a year or two diminishes with the number of natural predators, like that blue heron or kingfisher we fished with a few hours ago.

When we find ourselves in a joyous place, we humans tend to want to stop time, to arrest its passage. We know it's not possible, so we take photos, perhaps record the event in a diary or journal. Some hunters and anglers turn to taxidermy.

I've never had anything I've hunted or caught frozen in the amber of that ancient art. But as I hold this fish, smiling at Noah, both of us shaking our heads and laughing at the beauty of this anomaly, the luck of such a blessing, I immediately think about having it mounted, a version of life sculpted to carry with me through the coming days.

The temptation, though strong, is brief.

Her life is the stream. I have no right to take it.

She deserves another spawn, a last bit of summer before the blazing desire of autumn.

In opening my hands from around the belly of this ancient fish, in feeling her tail kick against my palms and watching her swim away, down and under the immensity of that boulder, I'm granted a vision. (Is it simply my imagination or does this elder, in her last touch, imprint upon me some of what she's seen?)

All I know is I find myself unexpectedly underwater. My ears fuzzy. Sounds of the forest far away. Noah's voice an indistinct hum.

And out before me the submerged logs that stretch another quarter mile up the stream.

And above the logjam, the long pool beneath hemlocks whose boughs dip the water if the flow is high enough, as it is today.

And the gravel where last year the redd was prepared in that ritual of love and longing for life to exist beyond our deaths. Where this female pushed her eggs. Where the milt settled. Where this past spring fry hatched, and all the fingerlings from the previous year darted, some to be engulfed by the mouths of larger fish.

And in some way, the past washes over me, through me, with its ice and snow, with its floods, with drought and logging, moving back toward a glacial time, an ice shield whose force pushed everything up in its path, and those first char, from whom this ancient mother-fish is descended, their memory deposited in her flesh, and now passed, even if incompletely, to me, simply because I've been granted the chance to hold her, to decide whether to release her.

And a glimpse of a possible future, too. A day in late October when I'll walk the bank looking for her, seeing her start the path of another generation with a swish of her tail. Giving thanks for her and what she taught me, helping me to fall even more deeply in love with her beauty, with the necessity of her existence, this water of life.

KACIE A. ENGLAND

A Circle Drive Obituary

My family died on Circle Drive in Jacobus, Pennsylvania. A dead-end street that is, ironically, situated at the bottom end of a Lutheran cemetery. The shabby single-family home where we met our inevitable demise was built in 1925. After speaking with Miss Hilda, the slipper-wearing, nightgown-flaunting keeper of all town secrets and chronicled criticism, we learned our house once belonged to the son of a turkey farmer, which explained why our quaint cottage looked almost identical to Miss Hilda's and the copy-cat house down on the corner. The farmer had called for houses to be built for his sons so that they remain close. The farmer's wishes might have worked for his family, but it didn't save ours from reluctantly fleeing the Drive.

Jacobus rested at the bottom of the state—smashed up against the Mason-Dixon line. If you were traveling from Maryland, deep hills littered with apple orchards and pin oaks eventually brought you into town. During the time of the turkey farmer, Jacobus was a Mecca for travelers. The tired voyager on their way to Harrisburg could stay, for a reasonable price, in the Jacobus Hotel on Main Street. But once they had their one-night stay, most were ready to return to the road and leave as seamlessly as they first arrived when they crossed the state line. The Circle Drive house in Jacobus also hugged a remarkable border—that of three cemeteries.

The closest of the three waited for you when the dead-end road turned from cracked pavement with clovers half-grown in the crevices to dust. My brother and I, not knowing what a bad omen this later proved to be, would run in between the graves, pulling kites behind us or petulantly chasing one another in a game of fervent tag. I can even recall a time when my mother, after frantic yelling up and down the Drive, had found my six-year-old brother sitting in on a grave-side service for a man we didn't know. When he skulked back home after attending the mystery man's funeral, and after my mom's half-hearted scolding and interrogation, my brother simply sniffed, "I'm really going to miss that guy." We'd become accustomed to, friendly, even, with the people who rested just six feet below where we stood in our bare feet and hand-me-downs. And I liked to think that they thought fondly of us in their postmortem slumbers. I now imagine them shaking their cold fists up toward the sky, trying to warn my brother and me about what awaits down the street.

What was meant to be my family's "starter home" both started and ended us. It was a small white house with dollhouse-like shutters that framed each drafty window. In the winter, when the glass would frost over, neighbors could see my finger-drawn sketches carved in the ice and stamped nose prints from Daisy, the yellow lab-border collie mutt we picked up one spring from an ad on *Craig's List.* Inside, each room was plastered in hickory paneling, my painstakingly crafted coloring sheets, and hardwood flooring that was so warped that you could see into the cellar if my mother had the light on downstairs. But despite this cold depiction, which one knows to be entirely truthful if they've ever experienced a Pennsylvania winter, my growing-up home was rather warm most of the time. At least, that's how I choose to remember it. The stone fireplace, which grew so thick with ivy on its exterior that it would creep into the chimney's crown, was lit almost every January night. And the mantle housed pictures of haphazardly thrown birthday parties and children jumping into piles of late October leaves. I know now that more warmth radiated from the photos than the hearth.

Such autumn days, eternally memorialized in wooden picture frames, capture some of my fondest memories of the dead-end road; it's almost as if our neighbors knew the Jacobus house was destined for something more sinister, as we were one of the most popular houses on the street every Halloween night. Pumpkins my mom would purchase from Brown's Market and then meticulously carve from the patterns seen in the grocery's *Home & Garden* magazine, which were always flipped through but never purchased, enveloped our front yard. And my dad would jump out of the homemade coffin he crafted specifically to spook brave trick-or-treaters. The wood he used to build the coffin was leftover lumber from the job site, and the pumpkin seeds were stowed away for next year's patch or roasted and gobbled up like the monsters we believed lived in the woods adjacent to our home and the cemetery. Not a scrap wasted. Evenings such as Halloween night, dressed up as that year's most ghoulish haunt, frolicking around town with the neighborhood kids, distracted us from the very ghosts that mulled about our home. After the jack-o'-lanterns were spent and we were tucked into our beds, strung out on Kit Kats from Miss Hilda, different ghosts haunted our halls. The moans of these ghosts sounded more reminiscent of my father's silent sobs, domestic howls, and my mother's pernicious boos.

And with further reflection, perhaps it's Pennsylvania's uncanny knack for seasonal amusement that helped me distract myself from my family's approaching death. Each Independence Day, Jacobus would host a Fourth of July street fair, which included everything from parades and tractor pulls to car shows and fireworks. My brother and I would ride our bikes from our dead-end street up to the main road littered with white vendor tents, five dollars in hand, and anxious to spend it all on a funnel cake or rip-off carnival games. A staple of this once-a-year event was the annual Miss Jacobus, Pennsylvania, USA Pageant—an amateur contest held on a makeshift truck-bed stage in the town park for girls aged three to twelve. The winner didn't take home a trophy or anything larger than a plastic crown and bragging rights, but something about the competition truly enthralled twelve-year-old me, and at the top of the age threshold, I chose to enter for my first and last time. My mother discouraged me, sharing that I'd probably be disappointed, but with my incessant protest, she reluctantly styled my lanky, scraped-kneed self in the most put-together outfit I owned—a terrycloth purple sun dress from the sale rack that season. And Miss Holly next door braided my hair into a clean, slicked-back do. After the judges, respectable men from our community, had grilled me and the much younger and rufflier and frillier contestants with questions about our favorite facets of our town and other Fourth of July frivolities, I learned the hard way that grown men don't care much for what you have to say once you're old enough to think for yourself. The fireworks looked different to me that year.

Despite all the diversions my parents sought after for us to mask our unavoidable downfall, it was inevitable that my brother and I would interpret our familial ending like a vague obituary in the *York Daily Record* or an unmarked headstone of one of our neighbors in the catty-corner cemetery. But in contrast to its insentient inhabitants, I always had a feeling that the Circle Drive house was sort of alive—that it somehow knew and cherished all my father's backlogged dreams that he kept in the shed out back or my mother's secrets stashed in the junk drawer. It had a hold on us as every good house does, and she tried to save us in defiance of all that happened to our disaster-bound descendants. My father had practically rebuilt the house from the ground up—a finished basement and attic, hand-dug ponds, a new porch swing, coats of paint, the nasty green carpet that stretched over our only bathroom like moss on the dogwoods torn up and out. My mother had a blueprint for what would make a perfect house and, subsequently, a home and family. My dad only knew how to sketch the plans for the former.

And it truly wasn't anyone's fault it worked out that way. We were cosmically bound to die on Circle Drive—kismet, even. Omen-led. There were generations of late water bill payments, broken bottles, and all other odds telling us so. And when my dad moved out during my fourteenth year, it was almost as if he slipped into a casket to be ceremonially cemented into the Lutheran graveyard rather than an apartment on Main Street. When the divorce was finalized, sealed with a new mailing address for my father, the dead-end house, the home that narrated the infamous demise of the family on Circle Drive, cried out, and death crept in.

MICHAEL GARRIGAN

Anthracite Country

Part One – Coney Island Special

You wander down the street across the railroad tracks that you gaze down and see a girl trying to ride her bike across so she doesn't fall into the sharp-side gravel, but she ends up just carrying it trying not to trip. You hold the door for an old gentleman who doesn't say a word to you through his fifth cigarette of the day. You walk in and see no menu. The lady behind the counter—she's been working here longer than you've been alive and now she owns the joint and her grandson is working the register and getting drinks and has to work this Thursday to pay for new tires for his truck—she asks you what you want and you say, "Two Dogs," and she asks, "Everything?," and you say, "Yup." She takes a long thin spatula and smears mustard and ketchup on the bun and places the hot dog in the cradle of condiment and smothers chili and onions on top, suffocating it. Her deft movements done without thinking creating the Coney Island Special. Her hands somehow stay clean. She wraps it in paper that grows translucent with silent grease. You thank her, pay, and walk back to your truck. The girl on the bike is gone, she must have escaped the avalanche of gravel. You can't remember exactly where your dad grew up, so you drive across the train tracks and take the first right. Your windows are open and the humid haze of July mixes with the dust of an old town making it hard to breathe. You hit a dead end at Shamokin Creek—named "place of eels" by the Lenape—that still runs burnt orange with acid mine drainage, lifeless, all the insects and fish drowned in chemicals. Your pap told your dad, who tells you, that back in the day when they heard a Prohibition Agent was on their way, F&S Brewery would open all their valves for all their tanks and there would be a three-foot head of beer on the creek as it ran through town. You wonder what the color of the creek was back then. You turn around in the parking lot of a closed corner store. A ripped tarp covers an open window. Siding is torn down, the houses row upon row in a stuttered line where the ground has begun to cave in or the roofs have started to sag, each street narrow enough just for one car but no One-Way signs. Some porches have people on them, some the banisters are falling, some are full of broken refrigerators and AC units. It's hot. There's a bar on each street, but also two churches. One used to be a Polish Catholic church that's now a Mosque. The hills are so steep your father must have been so damn strong to ride up them to the top to the coal mines where he used to play with the other kids.

Part Two – Culm Piles

My father, twelve years old and afraid of ripping holes in his only pair of jeans that his mother just bought him and would smack him good if she had to mend them already, tries to clamber out of the cascading, collapsing gravel of an abandoned coal mine. Surrounding the hole, valleys and ridges of anthracite butchered decades ago covered with ailanthus and sumac. His bitten down fingernails make scratches in the dried soil.

Every time he tries to grab hold, he slips a bit further and waits for the rock to settle until trying again—turning, grasping, chest scraping, slowing him down. Stop. He knows if this takes too long, if he can't climb out soon, his mother will be after him with a wooden spoon when he gets home. If he's lucky, his dad will still be at work. If he can't climb out, the gravel will protect him from that sharp crack, but he'll be hungry and hunger, right now, is more appealing than rest.

Decades later, he took me on a tour of the mines when I was a kid, roughly the same age he was sliding into that hole. We visited his grandfather, Poppy, lying in a starched hospital bed, skinny with near death. It was dark on the roads and in his room. The beige linoleum was worn dim like those hills, covered in soot. My father asked him to tell us stories. He did. When he was my age, he was one of the boys that would rob the pillars, setting explosives in crevices deep in the rock of the last columns of anthracite holding up the mine. Their tiny fingers were perfect for the job. They'd run as the fuse crackled and the explosion ruptured the rock. They'd wait for the dust to settle, counting the seconds to see if the mountain was done collapsing or if they'd have to run. Birds, mules, and fires were the marks of oxygen, of life. "If they went, you ran," he whispered. He counted to sixty and in that silence, he would wait. I was too young to ask what he did in that silent wait. But now I wonder—Did he play with the dirt between his fingers? Did he worry? Did rocks become toy trucks in those seconds of possible collapse?

My father inches up, dilates, holds still, waits again for the settle of the rock. Out of the corner of his eye, he sees a copse of hemlocks he thinks, growing tall enough to cover the coal equipment of Cameron Colliery, at the base of what was one of the tallest man-made mountains now a blackness spattered by dark helpless green. Tonight, if he doesn't get himself out, he will be left watching as Orion slides his way across a horizon cut with a rusted-out Bucyrus Erie dragline still reaching out, dangling its bucket over an open pit sore.

The coal and iron companies that once ran these collieries went bankrupt and left decades ago. They took the anthracite and the profit and left dead water and scraped hills. Some towns still burn, smoke comes up out of the cracked pavement. Some towns have museums open once a week. Most roads became dead ends. Most people drive hours out of the valley for work.

My father's hands finally find solid ground at the lip of the airhole. He pulls himself up and stands. His knees, bloodied through torn jeans, burn in thick summer air like dried leaves languid in diesel smoke. His arms are dirty, his shirt will need bleaching. His mother, my Nana, will scold him for this with that wooden spoon, but he's not thinking about that right now. He's hungry and no dinner served in this town will satiate that. He's skinny, tall and lanky like a birch growing out of shallow soil, but he will put meat on those bones eventually, just not here. He lifts the ball cap off his head, the yellow "P" faded on sweat-stained black, and his head full of hair catches the evening sun. He wipes the dirt from his cleft lip scar. He leaves the gravel and walks down the steep silent hill towards Shamokin Street, towards their two-bedroom row house full of Catholic guilt and forgiveness.

Years later, he keeps walking to another industrial belt town to get his degree in business then halfway back to settle near the Susquehanna

River. There he works for a company that nearly lays him off after thirty years, that makes him lay off his workers when they find cheaper labor overseas. I once visited his office. Two windows, a few trees lining a parking lot, nothing on the walls, an office he worked in for decades that looked like it was ready for a new employee to start the next day. "Ready to go whenever they say the word," he said. Forever dragging himself out of that abandoned mine shaft, working endlessly to provide for his family, never buried under rock.

Part Three – Roaring Creek (above the Shamokin Reservoir)

I was downstream releasing a brook trout when I heard a dog collar getting closer, then finding a new smell and turning away. There was nothing for it to hear of me. I had no sound to offer, just water around ankles. I came back here, just a few miles upstream of where my father spent his childhood, to catch a native brook trout that held the genes of centuries in its little body. One of the last few wild and native things left in this place. I wanted proof that this place was once wild, that it could be wild again. That something had survived. I strand myself out in the middle of streams as often as I can. I think of my father climbing out of that abandoned mine and his father pulling the family out of that town and his father dying from black lung. My hands drop, one free, one lightly grasping my fly rod, and I close my eyes and listen to the crashing, collapsing water that covers, but does not bury, become a silence that settles onto me, onto the bank, onto the clouds of bugs, onto the deep canopy of wood gripping the soil. Everything becomes a silence if given long enough.

CRISSANDRA GEORGE

Uncovering the Voices, Sounds, and Words of Rural Pennsylvanians

Rural PA is unknown to some, a drive to another more well-known destination for others, and to some, very lucky, individuals, it is called home. My view of rural PA can best be summed up by a poem I wrote in sixth grade that my parents joyfully sent to the local newspaper that they titled "A child's view of the valley," but eleven-year-old me knew the poem just simply as "Hawthorn, PA." I boast about the Red Bank River (which is known by locals as a "Red Bank *Crick*") and being the creative child I was, I even shaped the text of the poem to look like a flowing river. I explain how New Bethlehem, PA, the neighboring town, is filled with the scent of peanut butter from the local Smucker's Factory and how the wild strawberries around the area make the perfect addition to a tea party with my grandparents. The prompt for this writing assignment in class was to write about a place where you feel most comfortable. Looking back at this poem, one can begin to see how language and place are so interconnected, especially in rural regions of PA. The small distinct aspects that not everyone gets to indulge in, such as a peanut butter scented town or rivers and valleys that cover the beautiful region. The use of punctual whenever, a-prefixing, unique terms, and more heard in "Whenever I was a-fishin' in the crick" were not blissfully heard by everyone else. While my view of rural PA as a child was quaint and filled with comfort, my young adult view became more dynamic, and I yearned to see other areas and states. The curiosity of assuming there was more out there to explore than just rural PA flooded my brain, along with the comments from friends, family, and acquaintances insisting that "there isn't much around here" and "to get better opportunities, you have to leave."

A commonly heard and told story that all Northern Appalachians hear too often. The "child's view of this valley" was silenced and the desire to leave was louder than ever before. Little did I know that the voices and landscapes so familiar to me were so much more varied than I would have anticipated.

"You have no accent" was a normal encounter when I came to Mississippi from Pennsylvania for college. Granted, compared to other students, I believed that I truly did not have an accent (a wrong belief as I would learn through years of studying linguistics) and was immediately bombarded by a large range of Southern dialects that, at the time, were very new for someone from PA. Unphased by these comments, I remembered my friends and even teachers from PA saying "Oh watch! She is gonna come back with a Southern drawl like some Southern belle after the first year in Mississippi" as if how I spoke already (as well as everyone around me) was the opposite of "normal." These comments later began to come to the surface when I took my first Linguistics class. The professor continually discussed that "everyone has an accent" (better known as an idiolect) and explained regional dialectology and the field of sociolinguistics. My passion for language continued to grow as I learned about regional language features and how language and place are connected through speakers. Language is how we, as people, create boundaries, communicate, and understand the world around us. Previously, I had never thought about language in this way, and I had known very little about the field of linguistics, but when discussing regions of the US and their linguistic processes, I was stunned to only see PA mentioned a few times. It seemed as if the textbooks knew just as little as I did about the voices of Rural PA. Normally, any talk of PA Englishes was grouped with Philadelphia or Pittsburgh, none of which I could fully identify with as a rural Pennsylvanian. This lack of representation within these textbooks and lectures made me feel unseen. Classmates would see a feature used in Pittsburghese, such as "dahntahn" and asked if I, the only person from PA in the classroom, had that feature. I would reluctantly say no or that "I have heard it used, but I don't personally use it." This was a common encounter and response that I repeated many times. These countless situations made me wonder where were the voices of PA that I could relate to? Did my region just not have an accent like others have told me or was it not "unique" enough to show in textbooks? Were the speakers of this region just not special? These were the questions that I always pondered, but never got the opportunity to truly explore until graduate school.

After four years of studying linguistics in undergraduate and even working at a linguistic and cultural heritage project that specializes in collecting, organizing, preserving, and making accessible regional survey-style linguistic data, I made it my mission to find the special aspects of my region without association to the big cities. This began my investigation into Northern Appalachia, specifically focusing on Northern Appalachians from PA, which is still a new field of study in linguistics. Little did I know it would take an additional three years to figure out that historically, this region was understudied and the only source to consult was the people within the region themselves. Upon wanting to learn more about the language of my region, I attended graduate school in Kentucky, where I continued to work for the linguistic and cultural heritage project known as the Linguistic Atlas Project (LAP). While continuing this work and pursuing a master's degree in linguistics, I realized that I had two strong passions. One was to understand the language and culture of my region. The second was to collect, organize, and make accessible this information. Both passions resulted in my choice to also get a master's in library and information science, which gave me skills and tools that built upon my many years of studying linguistics. It gave me the ability to compile, process, and analyze efficiently all the LAP data from my home region, a task not previously completed. With this knowledge and preparation, I finally began to explore the language of rural PA that was so near and dear to my heart.

With data from the 1930s in hand, I began looking into interviews from rural Pennsylvanians. The field pages from lengthy survey-style interviews blew me away. I saw myself and my family represented. I even learned about other linguistic patterns occurring in PA in areas where I am from and from other regions in PA that never get studied. This data brought so much excitement to finally show to others my home, but this historical data was not enough. I wanted more. I craved more! If not for me, but for rural PA to finally be in a linguistics publication. Immediately, I began planning interviews with current rural PA speakers. Conducting these interviews was challenging, especially since I was living six hours away in Kentucky, but with academic exploration and critical inquiry leading the way, I would do anything to have this research come to life. I reached out to various universities in Pennsylvania, historical societies, researchers, even my own family members and friends. Through this process, I met many rural Pennsylvania researchers that continued to inspire this research. I felt a sense of belonging and community, something that I did not feel ever before as the only rural Pennsylvanian in most rooms, through inspiring conference presentations, outreach, and collaboration for future projects. It even inspired further investigation into my thesis data looking into rural PA speakers and their perception of their language and local identity. Finally, rural PA was going to be studied and analyzed. I was going to find out how my home shaped my language and regional identity.

The rural PA data was flooded with sounds, word construction, and sentence structures that were music to my ears. Common terms like "*warsh*" for "wash" and punctual whenever were frequently seen in both the past and present speakers. Terms for food and beverages like "pop," "scrapple," and more served as a melody that represented my region proudly. The use of a-prefixing ("a-singing and a-laughing"), double modals ("might could"), and non-standard past tense forms ("dived" and "clumb" for the past tense of "climb") were being actively used by speakers. Additionally, finding a community of rural PA scholars brought to light linguistic features that were not present within past data, but present across speakers today. Current speakers noted differences in meaning between "*creek*" and "*crick*" that was dependent on the size of the body of water, which was new to me. Even differences in the vowels for numbers like "one" and "two" were avidly noted. In both the data and community, some words or pronunciations were unfamiliar to me though, from areas of PA that I was unaware of, and my textbooks had never knew existed. Just as Pittsburghese speakers had well-known and advertised linguistic forms, so did areas of the coal region. "Ho But" (used to address others) and "bolio" (considered the champagne of the coal region) were commonly used terms and seen on mugs, shirts, and other items for sale. Acknowledged by other speakers, but never by textbooks. This use of language discussed by speakers showed what linguists call commodification and enregisterment, which indicates a deeper social meaning and identity-making through language. This identity-making showed perceptions of how speakers feel about their region. For example, in Erie, PA, signs and murals stating that "It's okay to love Erie" among other phrases, began to link the regional identity of the region to "insiders" and "outsiders," no matter if the perception is positive or negative. In the coal regions of PA, shirts and other products have displayed "I speak two languages: English and Coal," showing how the industry has shaped their lives and culture. This identity making shows linguistic perceptions of the diverse regional identities even within the same state. This can be traced through the history of PA with the influx of overlapping boundaries. The language of PA is a crossroads of east to west fanning migration, German influence, Dutch influence, Appalachian Englishes, Midland dialect boundaries, and more. PA Englishes is just as diverse as the region and people. These terms even vary from smaller contexts between specific towns or even the different industrial regions such as the bituminous and anthracite coal regions. Even reading the International Phonetic Alphabet (IPA) notations of the historic interviews brought a smile to my face, just as the present-day audio recordings used for the study did. I expected certain pronunciations and words, but what I did not expect was discursive comments on how rural Pennsylvanians used their world and their region to further define themselves.

Regional identity is a multi-dimensional and diverse topic. It can differ from person to person, region to region, or even on the specific context. Within my study, many participants discussed the variation between whether they felt a part of the region of Appalachia, the Midwest, Great Lakes Region, Rust Belt, or just a part of Pennsylvania. Some people even felt they belonged to multiple regions or that none of these regions represented their hometown. A large part of these discussions was also the stereotypes placed on the region with terms like "Pennsyltucky" and "Hillbilly country," used by rural Pennsylvanians, but they also made the distinction that this area could be a "different subset of Appalachia" when there are "honest and hardworking folk." Many participants even hint at the many industrial and economical situations that this area has faced, such as "wealthy outsiders destroying the land, going to the bank, and then never seen again" to show the environmental and socioeconomic devastation that this state faced whether it be the lumber, coal, oil, or steel industry. All these individual experiences and broader histories distinctly find themselves into the language of rural Pennsylvanians, further demonstrating the diversity across this localized place and space.

This study began as an investigation into the language of the region that I so deeply love and am connected to, but it also began a conversation. A conversation between the speakers of this region and how they define the area around them. Many participants contacted me after the interviews with more terms or examples they have seen in their everyday life that they did not mention during the interviews. Even to this day, people come to me with unique terms that they heard growing up or heard in their everyday life that have meaning to them and represent who they are. While this only begins to truly uncover this region outside of the major cities, it does show that rural Pennsylvania is a mix of beliefs, ideologies, and diverse people that deserve more focus to better represent and educate all who want to inquire about it. The many unique terms that come from a variety of regional influences from "*warsh*" for "wash" and the many terms for bodies of water, shows only the beginning of understanding this amazing rural region and diversity that consumes it.

JIMMY GUIGNARD

A Rye Sense of Place

Born in North Carolina, I always feel like an outsider in Pennsylvania. I absorbed the South the way I learned my accent—effortlessly, through a kind of cultural osmosis. My Southern knowledge and habits are a part of my DNA, like grits, barbecue, sweet tea, collard greens, and sweet corn. In the South, a lot of that corn makes its way into bourbon. I grew up with Maker's Mark and Wild Turkey 101, and a splash of one of those takes me home.

I've lived outside the South for over twenty years, seventeen of those in Pennsylvania, and I've realized I'll never soak up another place like I did the South. Which bothers me, because I like to know, really know, the place I live. I want to know the land, the seasons, the flora and fauna, the food traditions. The booze. I have to work to know Pennsylvania, and have learned the northcentral terrain and seasons from thousands of miles of cycling. At some point, I heard about the Whiskey Rebellion and started paying attention. After all, it involved whiskey, rye to be specific, and it's got a cool flag that doesn't adorn a Dodge Charger.

The Unofficial Tioga County PA Whiskey Co-Op was distilled in the flames of a northcentral Pennsylvania ritual I love—the fire ring. During the pandemic, Francis, Dan, Tom, and I started drinking whiskey regularly around a fire after our weekend bike rides. We avoided people, because the last thing a cyclist wants is a lung-scorching sickness. As the fire rings and COVID continued, we expanded our whiskey range from bourbon to rye. Our motto is "Your whiskey is my whiskey."

One post-ride fire ring, Francis brought Pikesville Rye. I found it a bit spicier than the bourbon, and I liked it. The whiskey seemed to match my attitude better than bourbon. I find as I get older, I'm a little less patient, a little more ornery, a little more likely to say "I ain't doing that." Later, I learned that Pikesville Rye is a Maryland-style rye, which means it is closer to bourbon than the hotter Pennsylvania and New York ryes. Pikesville Rye is a rye on training wheels, though a tasty one.

Then McKenzie Rye Whiskey from Finger Lakes Distilling in New York made the fire ring. Not a Keystone State rye, but the localest I could find at the time. Rye grains don't care about state lines anyway, just regions. The Co-Op started sending each other articles about rye and learned that Pennsylvania has a tradition of rye going back to the 1700s.

Rye whiskey makes sense in Pennsylvania. Rye is a hearty grain that survives harsh northern winters and cooler climates better than corn does. Back in the day, whiskey distillers had to largely stick to the grain that grew closest to home. These days, many distillers source their grains from anywhere, which has led to grains called VNS, for variety not sourced. Unlike wines, distilling whiskey requires more steps, which means, in the eyes of some whiskey experts, the grains matter less.

But some Pennsylvania distillers aren't buying it, and they have revived the market for local grains. Dick Stoll, the Stoll of Stoll & Wolfe Distillery, in Lititz, and Laura Fields, of the Delaware Valley Fields Foundation (more on them later), encouraged Penn State professor Greg Roth to borrow a few ounces of Rosen rye seeds from the federal government's seed bank and re-establish Rosen rye, popular in the 1700s. Roth succeeded, and, in 2019, Stoll & Wolfe began to distill limited quantities of whiskey from Rosen rye. Stoll had a chance to taste just one batch of Rosen rye whiskey before he died.

In this age of corporate this and hipster that, it's hard to get a true sense of a place. Unaged Pennsylvania ryes taste like 1792. History in a bottle, at once young and old. Roots in the Whiskey Rebellion that ran from 1791 to 1794 help make the connection. The Whiskey Rebellion grew out of farmers wanting to own the full worth of their rye, which they made from excess rye crops. Whiskey was portable and didn't rot. However, President George Washington and Treasurer Alexander Hamilton found themselves needing to pay for the Revolutionary War (another rebellion of sorts, I reckon). Hamilton asked Washington to levy an excise tax on the rye whiskey being produced in the Monongahela region of Pennsylvania. The excise tax was based on the capacity of the still rather than the amount produced, and the feds wanted their payment in cash, which farmers did not have. Whiskey was their cash. According to whiskey historian Clay Risen, stills were as common as barns in the early days of distilling, and the potential payout for the feds was huge. Of course, the farmers and distillers did not like Hamilton's plan, so they rebelled at paying, and Washington sent troops to enforce the tax. The farmers got mad, tarred and feathered a few tax collectors, flew some cool flags, and still didn't pay any taxes.

Many think the Whiskey Rebellion is the reason bourbon started being produced. I did until recently. The myth goes like this: the farmers in the Monongahela region high-tailed it south to Kentucky with their stills to avoid paying taxes. Corn grew better than rye there, so it became the grain of choice. And just like that—the Whiskey Rebellion gave us bourbon.

Except whiskey historians like Clay Risen and Laura Fields will tell you that's not accurate. What happened is even better. A few skedaddled to Kentucky, but most farmers disappeared into the hills around the Monongahela region and kept on making rye. Which reminds me of North Carolina moonshiners in the 1900s, without the souped-up cars. Nothing says rebel like spiriting your still away into the hills and carrying on.

My wife threw whiskey on the fire when she ordered me a bottle of Liberty Pole Spirits Bassett Town Whiskey, the taste of which set wheels in motion for a Pittsburgh trip and set me to wondering why there were no distilleries in northcentral Pennsylvania. An unaged rye, the label on my bottle says "aged a minimum of 1 days" (not a typo). I taste Pennsylvania in the rye, like I taste North Carolina in moonshine.

Bassett Town Whiskey carries a flavor with a little rebellion in it. The rye is not for someone looking for sweet. It's edgy, a little in-your-face. It demands attention. You don't have to like it, but you're not going to ignore it if you drink it. Unlike the South, whose history needs to be constantly smoothed over by good manners and sweet bourbons, Pennsylvania rye lays it out there. A gustatory rebellion that I can get behind. It's paradoxical that I find a style of rye that's trying to capture a 1700s spirit brings a stronger sense of belonging to my displaced twenty-first century Southern soul.

Francis and I juked our way through Steelers' fans picking through memorabilia, headed toward the Pennsylvania Libations shop in Pittsburgh's Strip District. The Steelers were playing the Ravens later, but all we cared about was Pennsylvania rye and answers. The night before, we had visited Wigle Distillery a couple of blocks away. Wigle makes good rye, but the place felt more hipster than rebellious to us old farts. Maybe it was the guy sitting next to us at the bar with the perfectly coifed beard and flawless flannel shirt. Maybe it was the guy on the tour with us who told us he came for the peach whiskey(!). Maybe it was the premixed cocktails sold in bottles. (A practice that goes back to the 1800s, turns out. Still don't seem right.) The place felt more CGI than analog. Since Pennsylvania Libations sold alcohol distilled only in Pennsylvania, we thought maybe they knew whether Monongahela rye referred to a region or a variety. I was hoping for some Stoll & Wolfe rye, a main player in the Pennsylvania rye whiskey renaissance.

We walked into a narrow room with bottles of whiskey, gin, vodka, and other alcohols lining shelves that ran from the floor to out of my six foot two reach. Toward the back, a salt-and-pepper-haired man with round glasses, a scarf around his neck, and a sociable vibe stood at a short bar. He asked, "Would you like to taste something?"

Francis said, "We're writing a story on Pennsylvania ryes. You got any of those?"

News to me that "we" were writing the story. I added, "We're looking for Stoll & Wolfe. We're interested in the history of Pennsylvania ryes."

I've got Stoll & Wolfe right here." Tony Merzlak set bottles of clear rye and aged rye on the counter and reached for a stack of small plastic cups. "You should try the clear rye first." I'd read the White Rye Whiskey was an attempt, like Bassett Town Whiskey, to capture the taste of the rye Hamilton wanted to tax. I took a sip, let it roll around in my mouth, and swallowed. Excellent. The Steelers fans in the streets became people hawking wares in the late 1700s. Electric lights became torches and oil lamps. Jerseys became waistcoats and breeches and long dresses tight at the waist. I felt a little closer to the spirit of Pennsylvania.

That hour in Pennsylvania Libations felt like one of our pandemic fire rings. Like any good whiskey drinker, Tony felt compelled to share, even pouring us some Liberty Pole after we told him we were headed there next. We left with two bottles of Stoll & Wolfe, a bottle of MLH Distillery's Monongahela Rye Whiskey, and a bottle of bourbon. (One of Tony's favs—it was superb.) We made him a member of the Co-Op, with all its non-existent benefits, then headed south toward Liberty Pole Spirits in Washington. We were feeling better about the trip, like we had found our people. Tony and his co-worker, Tessa Simpson, had assured us that Monongahela rye was a region, and Jim might be able to explain the lack of distilling in northcentral PA.

After a much-needed lunch stop, we walked into Liberty Pole Spirits, named after the liberty poles erected during the Whiskey Rebellion. There's a bar set to the right lined with six bottles of Liberty Pole Spirits. A Whiskey Rebellion flag hung to the left, its bald eagle clutching a red and white ribbon in its beak surrounded by thirteen stars on a blue background. An upside-down portrait of Alexander Hamilton hung behind the bar. Two men mixed drinks. Maybe ten people were drinking and talking and waiting for the Steelers game. "You Jim?" I said to the older one sporting a gray sweater, a grizzled beard, and crow's feet at the corners of his eyes. He nodded.

I ordered an old-fashioned, which was super. Jim said later the secret was burnt simple syrup. (Sounds simple to make but it's not. I tried.) I told him about my experience with Bassett Town, and he asked if I had tried the aged rye. Hearing my "no," he reached for the ubiquitous plastic cups. "You've got to try them in order. You can really taste what aging does to the whiskey."

I tasted the unaged rye, Hamilton's upside-down visage staring at me disapprovingly. I looked back at him, appreciating how helpless he looked, and glanced at the flag as the whiskey rolled across my tongue. I believe the eagle winked. After the Bassett Town left my palate, I tasted the aged rye. The rye tasted complex, older, wiser, but no less rebellious. "Wow," I said to Jim. "That's really something. Thanks." He nodded.

"So, why don't we have a distilling tradition up in northcentral PA?"

"I don't know," he said, "but I'll send you Laura Fields' email address. She knows a lot about the history of whiskey in Pennsylvania. She should be able to help."

"Thanks. Any chance we can tour the distillery?"

Jim waved us toward the back and said he'd join us after making a few more drinks. We strolled toward the rear of the former monuments company, admiring the pot still and fermenters and the overhead crane Jim said came in useful at times. We tasted some "white dog," whiskey fresh out of the still and destined to become Bassett Town. We looked at the barrels of whiskey aging downstairs and talked about how the location of a barrel affects the whiskey. Warm temps cause barrels to expand and suck the distillate into the wood while cool temps cause the barrel to contract and force the distillate back into the barrel. That process gives aged whiskey much of its flavor, and varying temps in a warehouse affect it. One barrel was crafted with clear "heads" or ends so people can see the amount of whiskey lost to evaporation, what distillers call the angel's share. Jim shared images of the new facility he and his sons were building to house their expanding operations. My mouth waters just thinking about it.

Back in Wellsboro, I emailed Laura Fields to ask her why there were no rye whiskey distillers around these parts. Laura started the Delaware Valley Fields Foundation to educate people about the issues facing small farmers, and she's the force behind the American Whiskey Convention. Laura has been researching Pennsylvania whiskey distilling for years. She says the "northern central part of the state was exposed to the disastrous effects of alcohol quite early on." Hunters and trappers of the time interacted with Native Americans frequently and did not care about the effects of the whiskey on the native population. Locals saw the effects of over-indulgence firsthand, which primed them for the temperance movements that spread in the latter part of the 1800s. Another issue involved the lack of railroads to haul grain in and whiskey out. Laura points out that there were sizable distilleries in Centre, Montour, and Lycoming counties in the 1800s, though those were affected by the demise of the logging industry and, later, Prohibition. Laura adds, "Too many people believe that rye was simply a precursor to bourbon, but that is far from the truth. Rye was different in almost every way a whiskey could be different. It's like comparing single malt scotch to a single grain whisky. There's a lot more implied in the name than just what it's made from."

Laura's mention of the temperance movement brought to mind George Washington Sears, Wellsboro's famous outdoor writer, better known as Nessmuk. Also a poet, Sears wrote a song called "Wellsboro as a Temperance Town" in which he claims that "The bar-rooms are like the dhry [sic] sand of Sahara." In another poem, "Lotos Eating," he sings the praises of rye, what he calls "the liquid cereal." It must have been hard for Nessmuk, nicknamed Bacchus, to survive the temperance movement. No wonder he argued that living in town was roughing it. The fact that he and I both like the outdoors, writing, and rye, however, brings me a stronger sense of belonging.

The weekend after the Pittsburgh trip, the Co-Op convened around a fire behind my house to taste some ryes. (My whiskey is your whiskey.) Snow covered the ground, and the Whiskey Rebellion flag hung from the shed. Venison chili simmered in the crock pot. Stoll & Wolfe White Rye Whiskey and Rye Whiskey, Liberty Pole Bassett Town Whiskey and Rye Whiskey, Wigle Rye Whiskey and Deep Cut Rye Whiskey, Dad's Hat Pennsylvania Rye Whiskey, and MLH Distillery's Monongahela Rye Whiskey represented the Commonwealth. We started with Liberty Pole Bassett Town and then moved to its rye. We did the same with Stoll & Wolfe—unaged rye to aged rye. We appreciated how the aging added complexity to the whiskey, though Tom said he preferred the unaged to the aged. (I have a warm spot for the unaged rye myself.) Dan threw more wood on the fire, his glove catching on fire at one point. (Maybe.) We talked for the umpteenth time about which hill in Tioga County is most difficult to climb on a bike. (For my money, Tiadaghton from the Pine Creek Rail Trail.) Firelight glinted in our whiskey glasses.

The next day, I walked down to the fire ring and felt the heat coming off the coals. Thought about the flames from the fire and the heat from the whiskey the night before. I appreciate how I bond with my friends and the land over rye whiskey. I appreciate how I forget about work invading my every waking moment, about being too busy, about Facebook and Twitter, about whether I'll ever be able to retire. I travel back to my early twenties don't-give-a-damn attitude, hard to capture in my mid-fifties, but which I like to visit from time to time. Don't get me wrong, though. I like my older self better. I'm a little more complex, maybe more spicy, a little angry. Like a good rye.

I'm proud of my Southern roots and appreciate a rebel spirit, but the Whiskey Rebellion flag hanging on the shed represents a rebellion that, unlike the Civil War, I can embrace without conflict. It's one thing to tar and feather a few tax collectors and then take to the hills to avoid paying taxes on homegrown hooch. It's another to fight to preserve slavery. I like rebellions involving whiskey.

I've got some distilleries yet to visit. Keir Family Distillery in Warren Center started selling rye in December (woo-hoo!), and Barrelhouse 6 in Hammondsport tempts me with its Brothers' 1910 Empire Rye. I'll keep imbibing my Northern home one splash at a time.

LILACE MELLIN GUIGNARD

Judging Distance

It's dark. I turned my headlamp off seconds ago as soon as I'd climbed up the ladder and gotten settled in my tree stand. All those years rock climbing out West are paying off in unexpected ways. I'm relaxed and comfortable sitting on a metal bench strapped to a trunk twenty feet off the ground—small pack clipped to the rail, loaded rifle with safety on resting across my lap. My first day deer hunting. Ever. I was raised in the DC suburbs with a love of the outdoors and a fear of guns. Though I've lived in rural Northcentral Pennsylvania for fifteen years, have happily cooked, served, and eaten venison given to us, have hiked and paddled and climbed in this landscape, today brings me closer to the land that's shaped me as a mother, the land that's nurtured my children.

My son, who started hunting last year in ninth grade, is probably climbing into his stand now. Jim, our mentor on whose land we're hunting, walked me to my stand before taking Gabe to his. Mine is closer to the house where Lori, Jim's wife, is preparing for the holidays. After spending the night in their loft, then sharing breakfast by the woodstove, I'm ensconced in the silence of the hills Jim has hunted since he was a kid. He built the house where they'd drop his uncle's truck at the pasture gate before heading into the woods. Jim has been generous with his time and skills. In addition, he and his father, Roger, share this land and the stands they've put up. Hunting is so important to them that sharing this activity brings them enough joy to offset the extra pressure we bring to the deer in this area. Jim's parents live down the hill, and between them they have the deed to more than thirty acres, with permission to hunt on adjacent properties. Only a fifteen-minute drive away, my husband and daughter are asleep and warm in the town of Wellsboro.

I look around, trying to make out details. It's as dark as inside the womb, I think, even though there's no way I'd know. The seam where sky meets valley slowly molts from black to deep blue. Behind and below me I hear Roger's four-wheeler pull up and shut off, then a few words with Jim who must be back at the house. Sound carries in the silent space. Roger heads uphill behind me to where his stand sits on the ridge. Jim heads inside to change for his weekday rotation of work at the funeral home. This will be the first opening day in ages that Jim has not been out hunting with his father because this year the season starts on a Saturday instead of the Monday after Thanksgiving. My son perches northeast of me, a little up from the creek.

Thinking about Jim going inside makes me realize I left my sandwich and baggy of mini chocolate bars in the fridge. Rookie move. At least I have my thermos of coffee. If I crane to one side and look behind the tree trunk, I can see the house lights (no shooting in that direction, obviously), so this time it's a mistake of low consequence. It was twenty-seven degrees when I left the house, the fire crackling reassuringly, and Gabe and I followed Jim up the hill. I wore my headlamp and heaviest layers, and while walking I felt like the kid in the *Christmas Story* movie who can barely move in his snowsuit. It wasn't a far walk. But, unlike every other time I'd done it, I couldn't see anything except the yellowish patch just ahead of my feet.

"Do you know where you are?" Jim asked. Instead of answering *no*, I raised my head to sweep my light. "See the straps?" I aimed my beam higher, recognized a landmark tree, and then, raising my head more, realized it was *the* landmark tree. I thanked Jim and wished Gabe luck.

At 5:30 this morning, when Gabe and I were groggily pulling on our layers, I had the rare chance to watch him stealthily. The umbers and green-browns of his well-used hunting clothes accented his dark brows and lighter brown hair. Handsome.

"Camouflage is your color," I told him.

"Camo's not a color, Mom," he replied as he headed for the stairs.

The blue bleeds into the low sky and honest-to-God light shoots from the ridgeline far above Gabe. Here we go. Shots sound to my left and right. I can't tell how close. I wait but hear no call from Gabe. Or Roger either. But, of course, it's Gabe's call I listen for.

* * *

Gabe started shooting with Jim one and a half years ago, at the end of eighth grade. I knew Jim and Lori from church. To say it was a tough year would be an understatement. I was aware it was the season children often grow distant, but I missed him upstairs in his land of Legos, door closed between us. He stood still twice a day and accepted my hugs, arms down at his sides, before he left for school and at bedtime. There had stopped being any response after my "I love you." His smile was an endangered species.

I wanted him to find an activity outside his room. Other than choir, he did nothing besides school, church, and create elaborate dioramas and stop action videos of military battles or zombie invasions. It didn't surprise or worry me that he wasn't into team sports. He'd done a few years of swim team and the tee-ball to instructional baseball stint, but like his father and me he preferred outdoor recreation. Unfortunately, there was no youth mountain biking team, though we were in a prime area for one. When he was twelve, he'd had a friend whose father took the boys shooting. Chris taught Gabe not to aim at anything he wasn't going to eat. I liked that attitude. After Gabe's first day of shooting, Chris told my husband and me, "Gabe could be a sniper."

Chris and his family moved soon after, but I kept reminding Gabe that if he wanted to shoot, I'd find someone to teach him. It couldn't be just anyone, but we knew people who met our standards. My husband had grown up in the South around guns. He'd shot some but never hunted. In my youth, guns meant shootings in the mall or inner-city gang violence. When out West for graduate school, I'd been exposed to hunters of an ethical and spiritual approach that I admired, but other than shooting a friend's handgun before our girls-only climbing trip, I was completely green. As in fresh, new, *and* as in Muir-aligned environmentalist. Not *Field & Stream* brown and green. As in Pennsylvania boy Pinchot-esque conservationist. As in the hook and bullet club.

Jim and I had had many a rousing exchange in adult Sunday school before I found out he was a hunter and that they lived outside of town with a shooting range in a ravine. Jim was enthusiastic when I mentioned Gabe might like to shoot. His sons are not interested in hunting. Now I had a name to attach to my offer, and soon Gabe responded that he'd like me to set up a time. My bait had worked.

At first, Gabe spent every other Sunday at the Wagner's house because Jim had every other weekend off from the funeral home. Soon Gabe was spending *every* Sunday there, playing card games or Pathfinder with Jim's older teenage sons, Gene and Isaac, even if he couldn't shoot. He'd leave church with them, and later Gene would drive the three boys back for youth group. Those evenings when he returned after 8 P.M. were the happiest I'd see Gabe all week. Knowing it was being at his second-family's house that made him so happy was the unpleasant aftertaste of a really good sip of beer that I learned to ignore. Mostly.

***

I've been mostly successful ignoring the cold, but now I double-check the safety, sling the .30-30 over my left shoulder, and pivot to my right to face the tree stand. Slowly, watching my numb boot-shod feet meet each rung, hopscotching my hands lower with each step, I climb down. Dried leaves crunch a bit as I gradually weight each step. I stretch and look up at the bare arms of red oaks and shagbark hickories, like the one I've been sitting against. In front of the tree and below my perch is a small open area where Jim has seen deer, and sign of them is left behind, such as muddy leaf-free patches on the ground and orange-ish slashes on low branches and trunks. Scrapes and rubs that tattle on the bucks that have passed through. The mast from these trees makes this a good winter forage area. Acorns and hickory nuts are mixed in with the dead leaves. It's a good spot to wait.

Gabe has a year of experience under his worn leather belt. For that reason, and possibly because Jim thought I might desire closer proximity to a bathroom, Gabe's spot is farther from the house. Being on private land that a limited number of hunters have access to, made me less anxious than last year when Gabe was doing an unfamiliar activity in an unfamiliar place. Unfamiliar to me. However, it was already a place he knew well, and this year, he is one of my guides, my experience with this terrain still inadequate for solo roaming. As I move about trying to get warm, I'm careful not to lose sight of my tree. I head for one of the few evergreens in the brown, a feathery-needled white pine under which grows some lovely moss. I send out thanks and apologies for using it as a place to stomp my feet back into sensation, something I couldn't do quietly on the dry leaves.

Warmer, I set my rifle down and move to an open spot where I push aside the duff, unclip my insulated overalls, and squat to pee. When done, I use my boot to spread the leaves back over the spot. According to my phone, it's ten o'clock, and I've been out three and a half hours. The temperature has warmed to the mid-thirties. Eventually, I head back to the stand for a cup of coffee. I want to make it till at least lunchtime before retrieving my food. Want to make Gabe proud.

The warmth of strong coffee on a cold day of hunting, twenty feet off the ground surrounded by the space and quiet of early winter woods, is a new adventure at fifty years old. I savor it. I study the hillside in front of me that rises steeply to where Roger sits. I know because I could see his orange cap from where I peed. Its clarity, even so far away that I can't make out any other details, is reassuring. I cup the last of the heat in my hands. Gray-brown tree trunks shoot skyward, with the softer brown of layered leaves filling the gaps in between and rising up until the trees merge with the far away top of the hill, becoming one dark mass. I watch a squirrel traverse tree-to-tree until I see the doe who's been standing in full view to my right for who knows how long. She is safe this week, but even next week she'll be safe from Gabe and me because we don't have antlerless tags. She has come from Gabe's direction and is feeding, head down. I lean back slowly and sip the last of my coffee, trying to figure out how far away she is.

Then I see—because now I know what to look for—her companion's head feeding just behind her. The body isn't visible, but the head is clearly a doe's. But where there are two does. . . . I'm on full animal alert now. The closest doe picks a spot for a nap just inside my little clearing. She delicately folds her front legs and then hind ones, dropping down with inhuman grace. Her head comes up and she seems to look right at me. Since she is up the hillside she's almost right across an airy gap from where I sit. But there's no recognition. When she lowers her head to curl it into her side I screw the cup-lid on as quietly as I'm capable, still holding my breath at the tiny *click*. Her ear twitches. I slowly reach left to where my open pack hangs and lower the thermos inside.

Now I scan the area behind the does where the distinct trunks blur into all that's beyond. Some of the blur is moving. I purposefully look away from the one bedded down and then back. I see her easily but only because I know she's there. The doe behind her is apparent only when moving or if a scrap of white ear, tail, or belly can be seen between brown posts. A memory comes of when Aunt LuAnn first showed me how to see green beans among the foliage. At first, I picked only a few, but once she showed me the texture and gesture to look for I found them unfailingly. There's a trick to softening the gaze that allows certain wanted details to stand out.

Now that I see what deer at this distance in these woods look like, it takes no time to spot the next one further back. The head movement is different—there's more area to it—which must mean . . . one step closer and I confirm it's a buck. It's still too far among the trees I think, but better to put the hammer back now. The safety, which makes no noise to switch off, stays on for now, but the hammer makes a light click no matter how slowly I move it. I raise the rifle and it doesn't take too long to find the buck in my scope. Not all of him, but I can see at least two tines before his head moves out of the circle I squint to keep in focus. A left-handed shooter, I brace my right arm against my chest holding the barrel up, following the buck as best I can, but he doesn't come into the open. Are there only two tines per side? I can't be sure, let alone see if there are brow tines. Any buck I shoot at has to have at least three points on one side. My arm shakes. I can't keep the antlers in the scope's circle. I can't confirm. I lower the rifle and watch as they browse around a cluster of trees behind where the first doe had been napping. The second doe follows the buck closely, but my doe, as I think of her, is more independent. When they circle back around, she comes lower than the others, but the buck will not be lured downhill closer to me, where I could see his antlers. Ultimately, she follows them over the lower rise back toward Gabe. It's noon. I wait thirty minutes more, scanning the blur behind the trees from shoulder to shoulder, until my growling stomach threatens to spook anything that ventures near.

***

At the end of my first pregnancy my stomach was huge. We knew Gabe would be big even before we knew he'd be late. Two weeks past the due date came and went, along with my husband's mother who'd flown across the country to stay five days in with us in Reno. Neither Gabe nor I would be rushed, both stubborn as hell. Our midwife checked in regularly, assured us he was still growing, still healthy, and left us with a way to frequently monitor his heart rate. Three weeks and two days after the due date, after drinking castor oil and orange juice to get things going, we ended up going with a cesarean section. I'd been in back labor for five days and once in the hospital even Pitocin didn't induce labor.

This is to say, there was a time when my son didn't want any distance between us. When he was a toddler, he once took my face in his hands after I'd tied his shoe and told me, "Mamma, I will never leave you." That long eighth-grade year and over the following summer, I recited these memories like a mantra or charm. Told myself not to scare him off, that only patience would bring him back in range.

***

Back out after lunch, I'm warm and full and aware this spells trouble. My sleepy time is after lunch, and here I am where nodding off poses a significant risk of breaking my neck. I know I should be scanning the woods, but my eyes are getting droopy from not focusing on anything. I look down at the rifle in my hands. It's Isaac's, practically the same gun as Gabe's. It's meant for a righty, though I shoot left-handed because the vision in my right eye is bad. So, while it's slightly awkward putting the safety on and off, using the lever action is the same regardless. It's a nice-looking rifle too, the wood grain smooth and handsome against my camo thighs.

These overalls were my last piece of hunting gear and took a long time to find. The day before Thanksgiving, I kept Gabe home (it was a half day) to help me in the kitchen and go to Cooper's Sporting Goods. We needed ammo and a sling for Isaac's gun, and while Gabe was looking for those, I browsed the two racks of clothing.

"I need bibs," I'd told Gabe in the car.

"Just call them overalls Mom. Bibs are what babies wear."

"But your father wears bibs."

"That's when he rides his bike," Gabe replied, as if Lycra and cycling was a different country from camo and hunting.

I like our local store and didn't want to travel an hour to an outlet. Here the men's overalls and coveralls were either too light or too heavy and thick for easy movement. The smallest they had was a medium anyway. Then I found a Kids XL on the other rack and threw my jacket and purse on the ground. When I pulled them over my jeans and clicked the shoulder buckles the man at the counter yelled, "Perfect!" And these were under fifty dollars instead of close to eighty.

Thank goodness I'm wearing them now. I scan the perimeter, jiggle my legs to get blood flowing. Nothing emerges from the edges. Gabe is somewhere over the little rise to the right, down a creek gully and up the other side. He is physically close. I assume I'd know if he needed me, but is that really the case? When he was in eighth grade, he was close. I saw him every day but couldn't tell what was going on. No communication. I'd talk to him about homework, grades, his attitude with teachers. No response. Before Gabe left for school he'd stand still as these tree trunks waiting for my arms to squeeze and let him go. Then he'd hug his father back and say, "Love you too" before walking out the door. Be glad for his bond with his father, I scolded my jealous heart. Be glad he has a family he can smile and laugh with on Sundays. Be glad and be patient.

I stalked him for a year before finding him again. And yes, I used whatever lure I thought might work. I got him hooked on shooting. I took him to Youth Field Day his last eligible year and marveled while he shot clays for the first time. Get those grades up, I told him, and you can get a rifle this summer. Screw around at school and you stay home on Sunday afternoons.

Someday, I hoped Gabe would look back and see *I* was the parent who made this possible. His liberal, poet mother. Not that his father didn't approve, he just didn't have the time or perhaps feel the same need I did to create these opportunities. Even though Gabe might feel he was escaping me spending so much time at Jim and Lori's, he was right where I wanted him. Safe, with good adults who loved him and set strong examples of respect and responsibility. I was pretty sure back then Gabe thought they were the opposite of his parents. In some unimportant ways they are, but I could talk to them and find out how he acted, what he said about school. They were a refuge he could wander safely in. The other days of the week I imagined his world away from me as a wilderness inhabited both by people who would do anything to help him and by people who supported a megalomaniac and didn't understand why brandishing the confederate flag was not okay. These were often the same people, making risk assessment difficult.

And when Gabe was home there was now a safe topic of conversation, one where I wasn't trying to scold or mold him. Who was at Sunday lunch? What guns did you shoot? From how far? What video games did you play? Each Sunday Lori invited me to come back too. Each Thursday at church choir Jim said, "Just let me know when you want to shoot with us." But I didn't want to ruin Gabe's refuge. Scare him back into hiding.

* * *

Much later as the sun is dipping low and the squirrels are playing tag, the buck comes up on my other side where the brush is a tangle. No does, and he's still concealed too much for me to count his tines through the briars and vines. He jumps, startled, when two squirrels make a ruckus beside him. I catch myself before laughing out loud. Someone must be moving, maybe Roger, because here comes a doe running downhill. The buck turns and takes off behind her. I look at my watch. Five o'clock. I follow their example and head downhill too.

I'm first back, already out of my gear, when Gabe shows up. We compare days.

"You must've spooked some deer around lunchtime," he tells me. "I saw two does and a buck run by from your direction. Only buck I saw all day. Didn't have a shot though."

I guess I didn't wait long enough before heading to lunch. "Did you get sleepy?" I ask. Last year he didn't hunt from a stand.

"A little. I got down and moved around. Could've walked right up to one doe. She had no clue I was there. Other than squirrels, that's about it."

We grab our bags from the loft and head home, sorry to have no stories but not sorry to have spent a fine day in the woods alone together.

* * *

In fall of Gabe's ninth grade, the first day of hunting season was rainy and cold, and the deer weren't moving. Jim describes the day as miserable,

"But he wouldn't come in," Jim says. "And the next morning, when I woke him around five A.M., he got right up without complaining." Gabe's good attitude was rewarded when he shot his buck late morning the second day. I found out by email. Tuesdays were a full day of teaching for me at the university, and I probably squealed when, between classes, I read the message: "What you want us to do with the deer." It'd been sent an hour earlier. How the heck did I know?

Since relocating, it's been made clear to me there are things that initiate a person into life here, that start the process of being "from" Tioga County. One is hitting a deer with your car. No one wants that to happen, but if you've lived here any amount of time it's practically inevitable. Our green Corolla checked that box years ago. The other things involve hunting, fishing, or tapping maple trees. When I stood at the classroom computer last year, watching my fiction writers take their seats, I felt our family's position relative to our home shift in a wonderful way. I told my students what Gabe had done, and they echoed my pride. I knew this wouldn't have happened other places I'd lived—either the hunting or this type of reaction.

With reservations, I posted the photo of Gabe with his buck on social media, but it was the best way to reach family and friends who would want to know. Gabe's expression is very serious. (No smile even then.) Many reactions fell along the lines of "Good man, feeding your family." Some didn't understand why it was necessary to post photos. Social media in fall is full of blaze orange posts with dead animals, and I understand the discomfort some of my friends feel. That had been me. But this was his moment.

Jim tells the story of Gabe taking the shot. The rain had turned to snow and, walking a bit to warm up, they finally found some deer far enough off that Jim pulled his binoculars out. Gabe kept his eye on them through his scope, both waiting for a clear view. "He waited for a long time holding the rifle up, never putting his finger on the trigger. When he said, 'It's a buck,' I said, 'Then shoot it.' He's got more trigger discipline than a lot of adults I've hunted with."

After his successful hunt, things got better with Gabe the second half of ninth grade (except for algebra class). He was talking with us more at home. Slowly he started seeking me out to give the requisite good night hug. I didn't have to hunt him down before his room went dark or miss my chance. That spring another man from church took Gabe turkey hunting and he got one. He'd insisted Gabe smile in the photo. It's a genuine one, rare and trophy-size.

One day when he was telling me about school, Gabe mentioned he was more country than some of the guys born here who wore camo and acted all cocky. "And *I* live in town," he added.

* * *

Sunday night Gabe and I are back over at Jim and Lori's. Jim has off the whole week, a yearly ritual. While Gabe can hunt Monday and Tuesday because our school district closes for hunters days, the university doesn't. I teach Tuesday/Thursday so Monday is it for me. It's snowing and I'm hoping to see tracks tomorrow. At their table, Jim, whom I haven't talked to since he dropped me at the tree stand two mornings ago, asks what I saw. I tell him about the buck and that I couldn't count the tines.

"What did you have your scope dialed at?" he asks.

"What did I what?" I have no idea what he's talking about.

Jim looks down at his hands, which are unwrapping bite-size candy bars and putting them in a baggie, shakes his head once with a pained expression. "I was afraid of that, but it didn't occur to me till I was at work."

"Scopes are adjustable?" I ask.

"Some are. That one is, and we had it set for shooting targets 100 yards out. The magnification was cranked too high for what you needed."

I knew that I was hoping to get a deer at fifty yards or closer. In these woods that's as far as I'm likely to see and have a clear shot.

"Made it harder to keep the whole head in the scope, get a good look as it moved." He sets the candy down and gets the rifle, showing me where the dial is and what to set it for.

* * *

At 6:15 A.M. we head in opposite directions in snow that's wet and heavy. The beam of my headlamp shows glimpses of an oddly familiar landscape, like the lamppost in the Narnia woods outside the wardrobe. Jim will walk Gabe to his stand, which is more difficult to find. I assure him

I'm fine, having gone back and forth from my stand to the house on my own several times two days ago. I've got the lay of the land now.

At 7 A.M. I text Lori: *still haven't found it.* I'm not worried, though I should've been there thirty minutes ago. I've followed deer tracks and watched a mole or mouse pop up and down out of the snow. I'm warm moving around, even though I move slow. I know I haven't covered too much ground because I keep going back and forth up the hill. The snow is so thick on everything I could be ten feet from the stand and not see it. My tracks fill in. There's enough light that I take my headlamp off. It's snowing harder.

I'm trying to get to the tree. I'm trying to make good decisions. I feel foolish, closing in on stupid, and don't want to ask for help finding my way. I push on with adolescent stubbornness. Yesterday I read a post on social media expressing the familiar sentiment that, if you give your kids a good base, then even if they go astray in their teen years, they'll come back to you.

I have my doubts. A good base helps, and we want to think this is true, but there are so many elements beyond our control. And even with the ones we *can* control, there's no guarantee our good intentions lead us to the best decisions. I've known good parents whose kids went too far in one direction or circled a bad choice too long to ever make it back. And I've taught students who, despite absent or selfish parents and the doubts they'd drilled into their children's heads, developed into responsible, likeable adults. Still, what we do as parents matters. Just only so much.

A pine tree. Rare spot of color in front of me. I remember marking three of them in view from my stand. Assuming this is one of them, and knowing I've erred to the west of my tree, I think I'm at my pee spot. I head downhill, deciding it's time to find the house and start again. Instead of coming out of the trees to the house, I hit scrub, so turn left. If I'm wrong, I'll hit the creek. If I'm right, I'll see the house. When I see the light Lori left on upstairs, I look uphill to my left and spot the tree stand. I text Lori: *Found it.* It's 7:30 A.M.

Sitting still, I get cold fast. My glasses are wet and useless. I take them off. What does it matter? I can't see anything. I've stuffed my wet gloves in my bib overalls and shake hand warmers, trying to get them heating faster. Every time snow falls from branches it sounds like a startled deer.

When it's just a small clump at a time plopping to the ground it sounds like muffled hooves. I try to remember all of the Robert Frost poem, "Stopping by Woods on a Snowy Evening." It's perfect iambic tetrameter. I get six lines in—a stanza-and-a-half—and can't remember what comes after the little horse. Is it a *little* horse or another adjective? I know it's two syllables because each line has eight syllables. How do other hunters keep their minds off the cold? Oh well. These woods are lovely, white, and deep.

* * *

Occasionally someone asks me if Gabe minds that I'm shooting and hunting now. Whether he feels encroached upon. These are always non-hunters who ask. At first, I was surprised at the question, not immediately remembering how I'd held back to give him space. By the end of ninth grade, Gabe had shot one deer and one turkey and provided his family with many meals—meat and stories we shared with friends. He'd started hugging me again, his "love you" returning like a favorite migratory bird who skipped a year. He'd found his way back. Instead of resenting my joining him in spring, Gabe stepped into the position of mentor to his mother. Watching him shoot showed me a young man who understood the responsibility a firearm requires, the patience and care. I was in a position to ask his help and if he didn't know, he didn't pretend to. The conversations he, Jim, and I had under the beeches and hemlocks surrounding the rifle range about politics, conservation, and theology are ones I'd have missed if I hadn't been willing to join him in his habitat.

For two weeks over the summer, while I was getting bi-weekly shooting lessons, Gabe and I were home alone together. Without schoolwork or anyone else around, we cut new trails of communication. Having seen how he handled a gun, I put him behind the wheel on empty back roads. It'd be soon enough he'd have his permit. Now he knew I trusted him with more responsibility, and he took on more at home. When we drove eleven hours down to North Carolina to meet up with everyone, we were easy companions. Talking a lot or not at all, finding common ground on music, listening to hunting podcasts. When my husband's father brought out the .30-30 that he'd only shot once, and gave it to Gabe, I was the parent there to see Gabe's reaction. He figured he'd be given the smaller .22. But a deer rifle was more than he'd hoped.

He's not thrilled that he isn't allowed to keep them at home yet. Our deal is he has to get all his grades into the B range before I buy a gun locker. Till then, they live at Jim and Lori's. It's not always easy, navigating the shifts between when he instructs me and when I parent him, yet I can't imagine what life would be like now if I hadn't learned to shoot. I'll never have the affection and admiration for guns, and the stamina to stay unmoving while cold, that Gabe has. But I admire who he is as an outdoorsman, and I proved I could wait when necessary, move in without startling him, and judge when it's okay to pull him close.

* * *

Today is the last day of the season, and while I'm caroling with my acapella group, Gabe is in the woods with Roger. Jim had to work, but he'd already filled his two tags (and his freezer).

I keep checking my phone to see if Lori texted with news. I'm bringing pizza by later to thank them for putting me and Gabe up each night before we hunted, sharing their land, their food, and their home. Also, because I can't let the season end with me in town. It's easy to answer "no" when people ask if I got a deer. It's harder to answer when they ask if I had any luck. Yes and no. Good and bad. I think about Jim's prayer one morning before we all headed out to hunt. "Father, keep us safe. And if it is your will that we get a deer today know that we are truly thankful. And if it is not your will, we are still truly thankful."

It's 3 P.M. when I get to their house. The dogs are excited another person is at the door. Gabe is already there, in front of the woodstove shucking out of wet clothes. It's been raining hard since noon. He was soaked and his scope was too fogged to see through. Gene is home from college so all three boys camp out at the table to play games.

"You got to keep it down out here. We're watching a movie," Lori tells them.

"Which one?" Isaac asks.

"A Hallmark Christmas movie," we say together and laugh when they groan. After a few pieces of pizza and several shushes they take the Monopoly board up to the loft, the dogs galumphing behind as far as the gate. We invited Roger over, but Lori said he was already in his PJs when she called. Each dog takes a turn lying on the loveseat with me. We aren't listening closely to the movie, talking about how nice it is when our kids don't hole up in their rooms, only coming out to eat and pee. On screen, the best friend of the prince admits to betraying him while elsewhere the princess goes into labor, just as Jim comes in and the dogs go crazy.

"What are you doing in here? It's still light out!" he jokes with me.

Later when the boys come down and Gabe and I prepare to leave, Isaac thanks me for the pizza and I thank him for loaning me his rifle. The dogs push between us looking for attention as we maneuver for hugs. This was the ritual I needed, a noisy house full of the smell of wood smoke, the voices of my friends, and the laughter and shouts of boys. Young men really.

"It was a great hunting season," Jim proclaims. "Everyone did it right." He looks at me and Gabe, nodding in his way that is mostly wise but a touch goofy. "No complaining. Everyone got out of bed on their own, dealt with whatever the weather was. A good season." While hunting is often a solitary activity, sharing the tradition with others is a big part of the culture. If it weren't, the skill would have died out instead of just declining.

We walk-slide down their steep driveway to where I parked. I ask Gabe if he's bummed he didn't get a deer.

"A little, but that's hunting."

I worried some last year that he might expect to always get something when he hunts, it all came so easily the first time. His response today makes me smile in the dark. His shape moves ahead, swifter and more sure-footed down the muddy hill, before he reaches the car. Some might think I didn't get anything my first hunting season. While I would've liked a deer, I did get something. For a moment I wonder what our relationship would be like if we didn't live where hunting is still a legacy passed along, even if, in this case, it's from son to mother. Then I shiver and hurry down to where he waits for me.

MICHAEL HARDIN

Build

On most Saturdays, you can find me in Milton, PA, working on a Habitat for Humanity site—helping to build a three-bedroom home for a young woman, her mother, and her three-year-old daughter. I have framed two walls, worked on the plumbing, built a back porch, and hung drywall. Habitat appreciates my talent. They are quick to praise, and if something is wrong, they provide constructive criticism on how to fix it or do better the next time. Volunteering makes me feel better about myself and about not having a job, something I never expected. Reluctantly, I am indebted to my father, the master builder.

The first project my father and I worked on was a small birdhouse. Okay, my contribution was negligible—I was four and held a toy hammer while my father built. This is how I learned—he worked and I watched. My father is a perfectionist. He beveled the sides so they fit snugly. He drilled a perfectly round hole for the bird, and he roofed the structure with leftover shingles from a burnt rental house he was rehabbing. Despite its flawless design and ideal location in our walnut tree, no bird ever nested in it.

For my father, construction required more expertise than demolition. Demolition could be entrusted to a four-year-old. On the burnt rental, he let me rip up singed roofing and pull off fire-scarred drywall. I liked the responsibility, although, in retrospect, I could ruin nothing. The worst I could do, fall off the roof. Nevertheless, I felt important carrying shingles and drywall to the dumpster.

My father did let me paint, which was a talent passed down from my great-grandfather, who painted bridges in Indiana during the Depression. I was given a wall and a roller and left to myself. However, my father painted the corners, trimmed the edges, and covered the floor with a canvas tarp. I was generally meticulous enough not to miss spots. "Roll in the same direction," he reminded me. "Up and down." I transformed the room from gray drywall to gleaming white. That made me proud. Then my father rolled over a spot that wasn't smooth. Maybe a nod. I waited for a "Good job, Mike." But no, and after fifty years, I've given up.

My father never taught my sister how to build. Working on a house was a sign of manly competency. I like being self-sufficient, not having to call a handyman or a contractor when something breaks. For that, I am indebted to my father, and the lessons have been hard-earned. Living in dorms and apartments, I did not need any tools. I did not even own a hammer or screwdriver. That troubled my father, so one Christmas he gave me a powder blue tool kit. When I opened it and noticed the label, "Do-It-Herself," my father insisted on getting me a "real" tool set. I refused. I liked the gender confusion, although the tools were sized for children. Nonetheless, I did not need to do any repairs or building, so the kit was perfect.

Eventually, during my Ph.D. program, my fiancée and I rented a house where most repairs were our responsibility, because the landlord lived out of state. My fiancée had been raised in a family where no one could fix anything, so that meant the upkeep was my job. I grew to like working with my hands, primarily because I was doing it for someone else. Left to my own devices, I would probably let everything slide. The most urgent problem was the bathtub-shower combo: the wood behind the tile had rotted. I had watched my father tile in the past, so I did as he had done, removing the tile and replacing the boards. In most cases, I can perform a task simply by having witnessed it once. I spread the adhesive, reattached the tiles, and grouted. No one would mistake it for a professional job, but it was good enough for that house.

After we earned our doctorates and married, my wife and I moved to rural Pennsylvania to teach. The housing market in Bloomsburg was dismal. Everything we saw in our price range had structural problems, so we expanded our search to Danville, where we bought a two-hundred-year-old brick farmhouse. Most of its weaknesses appeared cosmetic, things I believed I could fix. The orange carpet and green wallpaper in my wife's study got ripped out first. The padding had been glued down instead of stapled, forcing me to re-evaluate my competency. An employee at Home Depot suggested renting a drum sander, but big power tools intimidated me. I opted for a hand scraper and a belt sander, and over the span of a month, I scraped the padding off and then sanded the original hardwood floors made from hand-cut red oak boards. I varnished them and patched and painted the walls.

First room done. A gift for my wife.

Continuing slowly through the house, I pulled out carpet and varnished hardwoods. Most walls only needed cracks filled and a coat of paint. But the floors were not level, so in places the varnish pooled. In one room, the floor had been painted around the edges, hinting that a rug had once covered the center. Since part of the wood had been sealed for a hundred years and the other part left unpainted, the varnish absorbed inconsistently. All mistakes that my father noticed when my parents came to visit. I knew in advance the problems and watched as my father's eyes stopped at the imperfections. Silence. I could hear his voice in my head, commenting on each flaw.

Most of his criticism was unspoken, but on occasion he'd let slip. When removing the wallpaper from the baby room, I found slatted, horsehair and plaster walls in terrible condition. No choice since my pride and pocketbook prevented me from hiring a contractor. I hung drywall over them. While I could hang drywall, my weakness was filling in the seams with joint compound. I taped and mudded, but as hard as I tried, I could not get the wall perfectly smooth. In a few places, the tape was visible after I had sanded and painted. When my father saw this, he asked, "Did you paint over wallpaper?" I knew better than that.

When my wife became pregnant with our daughter, going upstairs to the bathroom became difficult for her. And so, one Thanksgiving, my father and I built a downstairs bathroom. As with the birdhouse, I mostly stood out of my father's way. He framed the wall, rerouted the electricity, and brought in the water lines. I watched. My father likes power tools, and so before he began, we made a trip to Home Depot where he bought a circular saw and an electric drill. He told me he would leave them here with me when the project was done, a gift. I tried to protest, this mix of too much testosterone and a fear of losing a finger, but I have never been able to assert my will with him. He would make a man out of me yet. I now have a love/hate relationship with power tools: they make the job easier, quicker, and better, but I have to acknowledge that my father was right. And of course, the bathroom was perfect and my wife was happy.

Besides the floors, the one project at the farmhouse that I felt best about was the deck that also served as a treehouse. I measured out a space next to a large maple and dug holes for the posts. I built it based on how I remember my father building a treehouse for my siblings and me when we were young. I dug six three-foot-deep holes, inserted four-by-fours, and filled them in with concrete. From there, I framed the floor and put down pressure-treated boards. I built steps and guardrails and even added a slide. The next summer, when my father came out, he saw it and said nothing. I could not detect any criticism in his eyes.

Having grown up working class, I know it is important to pass down this knowledge, so more recently, when I have projects, I ask my daughter to help. When I was stripping and varnishing the old mortise and tenon doors, my daughter helped me prepare them with a palm sander. I took a picture of her sanding and built a frame out of old wainscoting for it, including in it a picture of me at four, holding my hammer next to the birdhouse. I gave it to my father so he could see how his legacy had been passed down. He hung it in the hallway of his house. For me, teaching my daughter is important so that she does not have to feel dependent on a man for anything. I am also trying to teach my son how to build and fix things, but that seems less urgent. I don't want to impose a masculinity upon him. I want him to ask me if he can watch or help.

Sometimes, when I am working on a project, I'll ask him to drill in a screw. He likes to be helpful but does not seem to want to know much more.

So for now, I work for Habitat with a crew of older guys who remind me of my father. I am the go-to fix-it guy for my wife's friends and church. My father will never see this work. And we have moved into a modern home, without the problems of an old farmhouse. Mostly, what I do at home is replace light fixtures, paint, and occasionally tile. Nothing complicated, nothing to be noticed. Part of me misses the projects with my father, the way we could wordlessly transform a room. But another part of me is happy not to have the finished product reminding me that what I am best at is holding a hammer and smiling.

PATRICK THOMAS HENRY

Playing in the Lost Woods: Splinters and Pixels

It's Dangerous . . .

The scoutmaster cracked open a beer on the lip of the old hob stove in the troop's cabin on Mount Wopsononock. The other scouts—including my two older brothers—were outside, hundreds of yards from the cabin, scouring the clearings between the gnarled pines and the boughs of mountain laurel for patches level and clear enough for our tents.

It was autumn—cold, the fallen leaves fringed with frost. But there wasn't snow, not yet. It was, as the troop leaders told us, prime training for the Penn's Woods Council Winter Jamboree. The scouts would sleep outside. The scoutmaster and the leaders would bunk in the cabin—with the woodstove, with plumbing, with sturdy beds.

The scoutmaster smacked his lips. He'd emptied the beer. He wanted to talk to me, he said. I didn't hunt. Or fish. Or hike. Or play football. Or run track. His son said I was one of those geeks, happier with a book or a Nintendo controller in my hands. He said, "You don't know how to appreciate the spirit of the woods."

Something howled outside and he slapped his thigh. "We got coyotes out there!"

Except it wasn't coyotes. Beyond us, in the depths of the woods, the older scouts were vaulting and springing from the boughs of mountain laurel, fencing with rotten sticks, and pelting each other with fat clods of moss.

***

The scoutmaster wasn't entirely wrong. I was happier in the pixelated forests of video games than I was at campouts and troop outings. In

Nintendo's *The Legend of Zelda* franchise, a series of action-adventure games in which the player takes control of a boy named Link, gamers wander through the forests and mountains of Hyrule, seeking out the ancient golden triangles imbued with the power of Hyrule's creator goddesses—the Triforce. As Link, a hero clad in a green tunic and pixie hat, the player protects the Princess Zelda, helps her protect the Triforce, and prevents it from falling into the hands of the evil sorcerer, Ganon.

In a franchise that includes nearly thirty games, across multiple franchises, *Zelda* charts out forests realer than the forced camaraderie and bullying of scout camp. Woodlands that plead for exploration. For meditation. For wonder.

* * *

I've been told my memory is impossible, a cluttered tacklebox of hooks and line, as likely to snag on something sensitive and rip out an old sinew that time should've healed. I've been told that I can't possibly remember the odd snatches of images trawled in my mind—like endless rounds of rock-paper-scissor that my brothers and I played to determine who got to play the new Nintendo Entertainment System and who got stuck on our father's burned-out Atari.

These are tangled in the net; I know I remember them, no matter how often I'm told that I've simply pasted together snippets of overheard conversation.

Another memory, thrashing its tail and binding itself with the others: April of 1990, around the time of my fourth birthday, on the back deck of my grandparents' house in Big Run. Nearby, under an olive-drab canopy, stood the prop canon that my grandfather had forged and constructed for a Revolutionary War reenactment during the bicentennial. My grandmother handed me a shiny green gift bag that sprouted pastel sprigs of paper; she loathed wrapping packages, the fuss of tape and creases, all that measuring and cutting. I shucked the paper from the bag, pulled out a golden box with a silver shield embossed on its cover. A small cutout in the shield revealed the golden bars on the grip of a game cartridge. *The Legend of Zelda*, for the Nintendo Entertainment System. Released in 1986, the same year I was born.

I ripped the plastic wrapping from the box. I stared into the forest, up the hill from my grandparents' house, where foxes sometimes emerged to scavenge the berries from the low briar bushes. And I'm certain, one peered down the hill, stared me down, invited me to chase it into the hills. Even though we were always told: it's dangerous to play in the woods; it's dangerous to be alone in the woods.

The fox and *Zelda*: *Zelda* and the fox and their mutual promise of adventure, in the forests of Pennsylvania. It has the force of truth. But are these birthday memories really entwined? Did I truly see a fox, passing between the broad trunks at the tree line? Or has my memory mapped it there, layered it on the pentimento of so many other encounters, so many other blazes of foliage and fur charred into my memory, like the ghosts of dead images seared into the screen of an old cathode-ray tube television?

* * *

Because I was detained to listen to the scoutmaster's monologue on masculinity and the spirit of the woods, the tents were filled and I knew better than to plead for a spot with one of my brothers. (Like all teenaged brothers, we were privately friends, but antagonists in public.) The troop had abandoned my backpack at the tailgate of a rusted-out Bronco. It had been raided—my electric lantern stripped of its battery, the snap-activated hand warmers fleeced but the packaging left behind, a box of strike-anywheres left emptied. Even the foam for under my sleeping bag was nabbed.

They hadn't found the secret pocket in my backpack. My Game Boy Pocket with a cache of AAAs, a *Zelda* game, and a few bright glowsticks: I'd manage for the night.

I slung my pack onto one shoulder, scooped up the last remaining tent bag. By the remote blink of the other scouts' fires, I navigated toward their camp spots, then halted. The air crackled, from cold and the distant snap of logs. I reversed course and set out in the opposite direction. The porchlight of the cabin on Wopsy became an inverted Polaris—something I glanced over my shoulder for, to keep my bearings, but something I wanted to remain forever behind me.

Inside the tent, by a glowstick's light, I played *Zelda* for hours. The scoutmaster had thwarted nothing.

* * *

In elementary and middle school, we read short stories and novels of adventure, of abandonment in the forests. Gary Paulson's *The Hatchet*, Jack London's "To Light a Fire," Jean Craighead George's *Julie of the Wolves* and *My Side of the Mountain*. (My teachers always pointed out that George had graduated from Penn State in the 1940s: even if she was writing about Alaska or the Catskills, she was local—State College was an hour drive from Bellwood, unless you sped like the tailgaters careening to game day at Beaver Stadium.)

The wildernesses of these stories beleaguered their young protagonists, threw waves of vile weather and ravenous beasts and the braided threats of starvation and dehydration. The protagonists survived—or died—by their wiles.

The schoolkids in camouflage took the stories as a zero-sum game: you live or you die, there's no in-between.

But I read something else: every trail in these lost woods wound towards introspection or discovery. The fictional forests and the real ones were, in my mind, twins. In the margins of notebooks and handouts, I doodled scenes of Link at a campfire, Link setting traps, Link fishing in a river. Surely, to survive in the forests of Hyrule, Link had to explore and hunt and scavenge and build campfires, like so many adventure-story heroes.

* * *

On the first screen of *The Legend of Zelda*, the player finds Link, the pixelated elf, on a well-tramped, beige field. One of the moss-furzed walls contains a black cutout—the entrance to a cave. Inside, an old man offers Link a sword with a green hilt and a maple-brown blade. "It's dangerous to go alone," the old man says. "Take this."

The manual calls the weapon, simply, the "sword." But we always saw it for its true self: a child's plaything, a wooden sword.

* * *

Spring semester, my sophomore year at Susquehanna University, finals week. I power on my flip phone after turning in my statistics final, and it immediately judders in my palm: several missed calls, a litany of texts, a full missal of voicemails. All from Joe, my oldest brother, a Marine Corps reservist who worked nights in an Outback kitchen and weekends as a mechanic. Joe's texts chant out one of his recent finds at Zerns, the farmers' market and auction house in Gilbertsville. A copy of the Nintendo 64 masterpiece, *The Legend of Zelda: Ocarina of Time*, with a weird label. All black and grey, tendrils of smoke.

His voicemails resonated, tinny and cavernous: recorded on speakerphone as he drove, the messages copied the rattle of his phone in the cupholder. First he was rolling from Reading, ready to chuck the defective cart right at the seller's jaw. No: the highway was blocked, he was pulling a u-ey and hookshotting back around. He was driving to me. Then he was beyond Harrisburg, the opal replica of the Statue of Liberty lifting her torch from the crags in the Susquehanna. Then he was flipping off the sign for Doctor Tom's Leather, where US-11/15 flanked the Susquehanna. Then he was at the Sheetz north of Selinsgrove, pounding a pretzel melt and a Dr Pepper because *fuck, was he still hung over and pissed to boot.*

In his last voicemail, he said: *I'm gonna toss this fucker in the Susquehanna.*

I run from Fisher Hall, through the threads of finals-zombified students trudging through the haze between exams, to my little Saturn station wagon, parked behind my dorm. I take University Ave at the speed limit but daydream of blazing down the road at fifty, ignoring the stop signs and the traffic light at Market. I take things slow, legally: I have always feared the cops, feared tickets, feared traffic stops, feared the smell of polished leather emanating from their holsters and the boot-polish threat of their sidearms and their scoutmaster-smug grins. I crossed Market Street, took the road east at a steady fifteen miles-per. Even at that speed, the wheels zithered over the old grate bridge connecting Selinsgrove proper to the Isle of Que.

I veer towards a curb and knock my chin against the top of the steering wheel when the tires rut over a curb. I stop inches shy of the brick sidewalk. Down a hill, at the water's edge, stands Joe. Oil dollops the fanned collar of his mechanic's tunic—peanut oil from a deep frier or something dredged from the guts of a blown-to-shit Ford, I can't tell. Beyond him, beyond the river and the ducks jittering on the water like the shivering figurines on the tin turf of an electric football table, darkness wells under the wall of conifers and old deciduous growth.

I stumble out of the car, toss the door shut behind me, and scrabble down the embankment—toward the Susquehanna, toward my brother.

I reach Joe in time to grab him by the elbow, as his arm pitches back, ready to pass the game cartridge deep into the Susquehanna, that river of the long reach. He fumbles the cartridge, and it tumbles to the dirt.

* * *

Another memory, thrashing in the net: Grandma sewing us costumes, as our aunts laid a transparent graph over a contour map of the hills around Big Run. Our grandfather, Pop-Pop, pulling a red robe over his head and hooking a fake beard, manufactured from polyester batting, around his ears. Grandma passing Pop-Pop a stack of three-by-five cards: his messages and warnings and hints, all written by Grandma. Three wooden swords unsheathed on the concrete slab of the back patio. A promise to guide us through the forests and into the dungeon. A path through the blackberry bushes, past the narrow mouths of the rabbit burrows, beyond the old birch split by lightning. A vow, that we wouldn't get lost in the woods.

A game engineered by our grandparents, a *Zelda* adventure in their woods. There, the memory ends: no flash of fox fur, or soundbites of dialogue, or cryptic wisdom dispensed by Pop-Pop in his guise as the Old Man. The Lost Woods awaited.

* * *

Most games in the *Zelda* series feature a forest called the Lost Woods. Here, the repeating pattern of trees misdirects the player. Monsters or bandits, with all the aggression of adolescent Boy Scouts, leap from the trees and imperil Link. You can wander infinitely, seeking the exit.

But there is always a safety valve, always a release: go east one screen to return to the main map of Hyrule, or turn around and return to the village. You may not have solved the maze, but you made it out alive.

* * *

On our first trip together to Zerns, Joe buys a slew of camera lenses, a couple of Coke bottles, and antique oil cans. He guides me through the stalls, where I find a vendor with racks of games. I only have twenty-five bucks, cash; my debit card is pointless, the account always zeroed out. I buy a small hoard of Super Nintendo games—*Super Mario All-Stars + World*, *Super Mario RPG*, *Star Fox*, *Street Fighter 2*, a couple of others.

In less than a decade, several of these games will cost a hundred bucks or more *each*. In the moment, all I care about is that they're cheap—a dollar or two each, for loose cartridges. I buy as many as I can afford. In hindsight, I should've nabbed that vendor's complete-in-box copy of *The Legend of Zelda: A Link to the Past*. But I need a little cash left over, for the used booksellers in Zerns and for a Coke and sandwich from the food stalls.

When Joe asks if I thought this place was the shit, I say, simply, "Yeah."

***

In the eighth dungeon in *The Legend of Zelda*, the old man reappears in a remote, dark room. To Link, he says, "Spectacle Rock is an entrance to death."

The cryptic riddle sets Link off to Death Mountain, where a pair of massive boulders resemble a pair of eyeglasses. By detonating a bomb before the left one, Link reveals the hidden entrance to the final labyrinth—the layer of the sorcerer Ganon, who seeks to control all of Hyrule.

I can never un-see the legacy of that riddle: building faces with windows resembling eyes, the troop's cabin high on Mount Wopsy. All entrances to death. But sometimes death is a metaphor, a productive force. Sometimes death generates life and art.

. . . to Go Alone . . .

"Out here," Porochista Khakpour writes, in the first paragraph of her short story "The Deer-Vehicle Collision Survivors Support Group," "we have only ourselves."

It might be the most Pennsylvanian sentence I've ever read: solitary, resilient, tinged with catastrophe.

***

During my junior year at Susquehanna, I call Joe and ask him about that camping trip, about the scoutmaster, about Wopsy.

"That guy was a dick," Joe says. But he remembers that campout. And he adds something to the memory: apparently, after I'd set up my tent and managed a small fire of my own, I patrolled my small patch of woods with a glowstick, overturned rocks, hunted for secret portals or buried trinkets.

Joe tells me this. "I found a two-by-four with a pair of nails in it and told the rest of those shitheads to leave you the fuck alone."

"Thanks," I say.

* * *

When he was a child in the late 1950s and early 1960s, the legendary video game designer Shigeru Miyamoto had little by way of toys in the rural village of Sonobe. He equipped himself with a stick and slashed his way through the bamboo growths and cedars and pines behind the village's Shinto temple. In the hillsides he found a cave, which contained nothing but darkness.

Miyamoto returned the next day, with a lantern in hand. He shimmied himself into the narrow aperture of the cave's mouth. Once inside, his lantern illuminated the cave, cast its pale light along the dark blots of other tunnels, other chambers.

True or not, this is the story Miyamoto tells about the creation of *The Legend of Zelda*, his own original game of rural exploration, of lonely wandering in the woods.

* * *

Months after Joe nearly hurled the copy of *Zelda: Ocarina of Time* into the Susquehanna, I googled alternate labels and editions of the game. I was alone in my dorm room; my roommate, as ever, was out drinking with friends.

Joe's copy, with its grey label and its tendrils of ominous smoke, matches the Japanese release of the game. How this cartridge got from Japan to Pennsylvania was a secret to everybody.

* * *

The night after I camped alone and remote from the other scouts, the forest was littered with snapped branches, saplings tramped down to pulp, massive clods of moss and dirt strewn about. One boy had to bandage his forearm. Another had a blackberry-dark bruise, striped across his forehead. A perfect welt.

You missed a real hell of a swordfight, the other scouts said.

Thought I wasn't involved in the melee, the scoutmaster tasked me with collecting the snapped and splintered sticks, all those decimated wooden swords. They'd make good kindling.

Sure, I thought: incinerate any sense of play. The Boy Scouts always made for perfect misery.

* * *

During my senior year at Susquehanna, Joe ships out to Iraq. In letters, he asks for Magic: The Gathering cards, pre-paid phone cards, cash, freeze-dried fruit, instant coffee. The damn churches send the Marines too many fucking carbs and too much peanut butter and chocolate. Over the phone, Joe tells me that all that dough and sugar melts to fucking super glue and it welds your goddamned mouth shut.

After grousing about the care packages, he requests a favor. "Don't do it if it's out of the way, though."

"What is it?"

"Go to Wopsy and take some pictures for me. I want to show some of the guys the cabin. I want to see a little green."

"I'll see what I can manage."

* * *

I return to Zerns first, by myself. I find a copy, complete-in-box, of *The Legend of Zelda: The Minish Cap* for the Game Boy Advance. In this game's version of the enchanted Lost Woods, Link must shrink down to the size of a thimble to navigate the hidden peepholes and knots of fallen logs, to travel upon lily pads across bodies of water, to collect the secret pebbles and gems scattered throughout the woods.

I've grown up, and so has the *Zelda* series. And around us Pennsylvania remains wild, untamed. Pennsylvania, too, demands us: shrink down to child-size, and enter the woods.

* * *

During spring the weather on Mount Wopsy is fit only for gnats. I drive up PA-865, following a half sheet of directions that had survived high school, stuffed into the back pocket of a Trapper Keeper. I burn through three different Billy Joel cassettes on my car's tape deck, searching for the turns and half-remembered signs—a deer-crossing sign (everywhere, in Pennsylvania), an access gate, a taxidermist's shop.

If only it were as easy to find the old turn-off for the camp, as it is to open a pad of graph paper on your lap and draw out dungeon maps while playing *Zelda*. But I have three rolls of color film and one of Joe's Canon cameras and I'm going to get some pictures, damnit.

Long before I find the camp, I get lost on Wopsy, on an old logging trail barely wide enough for my Saturn station wagon. At the path's end stands a shack, its planks rotten. Its door droops from its frame. The narrow windows on the shack's face resemble a pair of fractured, wireframe eyeglasses. Inside, I discover a cot, a deer skull mounted on the wall, and a stack of photo plates decayed beyond recognition.

I take photos that I'll send to Joe, along with the negatives. The package never reaches him—abandoned or filtered or intercepted, somewhere in the military mail bags.

The shack on Mount Wopsy, with its twin windows and their cracked-spectacle look, yielded a poem. An odd assemblage of craft ruminations and Pennsylvania grit. Perhaps I'll share that lyric, someday.

* * *

The last time I saw my grandfather alive was my parents' wedding vow renewal, in June 2011. I propped his body against mine, served as his crutch down the stairwells in the Methodist church. Even on oxygen, with his lungs giving out, he refused the stairlifts. He muttered about trekking in Alaska: he was deployed there during the 1950s, ran tank and assault vehicle trainings, and—famously, in our family—photographed a pair of brawling Kodiak bears.

I fetched Pop-Pop a plate—a sandwich, some vegetables, a slice of blueberry pie. He stabbed at the pie first. Juice from the berries caught on his shirt collar, his tie. The purple blots matched those on his cheeks, the backs of his hand. Oxygen deprivation. He grappled my wrist and hauled me in close.

"Francis," he said. My grandmother's older brother, Pop-Pop's childhood best friend. He was speaking to a ghost. "Francis," he said again. And then he whispered: a path through the woods, past a forked tree, down into a gully, cross the stream, to the secret place. Francis, he said, would remember the secret place from the rocks they rolled there—a seat for each of them.

Their own little spectacle rock, I'd conclude, but only later. I listened. I tried to explain that I wasn't Francis. But he kept speaking of the "secret place," the stone seats, their conversations.

I would never make sense of the directions, would never decipher the route. And I would never have the chance to ask him for another hint, a cryptic clue like "Tenth enemy has the bomb" or "If you go in the direction of the arrow" or "Spectacle Rock is an entrance to death"—all of those clues that *Zelda*'s old man dispenses. A day after my parents' wedding vow renewal, my grandfather died—in his own home in Big Run, surrounded by the Jefferson County forests that he taught us to explore.

Take This.

You're never lost in the Lost Woods, not truly. There is always a solution to the mazes in these pixelated forests. In *The Legend of Zelda*, travel north one screen, then west, then south, then west: the Lost Woods eject you at the mouth of a cemetery, populated with cackling, one-eyed ghosts capable of moving only in a grid-like pattern, like the rooks on a chessboard. In *Ocarina of Time*, follow the music, and the Lost Woods conduct you—with a tinny ocarina ditty fluting in your ears—to a vast glen, where a temple of ancient mysteries waits for your childhood to extinguish, waits for you to become an adult wise enough to fear the shadows but brash enough to crave their secrets.

* * *

In the introduction to his collected *Early Stories: 1953–1975*, Shillington native John Updike writes of leaving Pennsylvania for Massachusetts: "I arrived in New England with a Pennsylvania upbringing to write out of my system." In a conversation with Donald Hall, Marianne Moore—who grew up in Carlisle and graduated from Bryn Mawr—agreed with Hall that her life in Pennsylvania had kept her "isolated from modern poetry."

How unimaginative, to render Pennsylvania as a place to escape, or as a prison of the mind. How unimaginative, to dream of Pennsylvania as anything but an otherworld of magic and mystery, carried with us, wherever we go.

* * *

Several years after the release of *Ocarina of Time*, I spent a week of my summer with my grandparents. I was already planning out the Halloween costume I'd wear in Bellwood's annual parade; members of the high school marching band, like myself, were expected to be in costume. I would dress as Link, of course. "It's not just the clothes," Grandma, still the costumer, said. "You'll need to have his sword and shield."

Pop-Pop and I descended the stairwell, down into the garage and the woodshop in the cellar-level of the house. With a print-off of Link's blue-and-silver shield and a toy replica, he drew out its shape on stencil paper, drafted up a cut list, ran pieces of plyboard through the table saw, and navigated the curved pieces on his bandsaw. With a biscuit-joiner he assembled the sections. Together, we drew the design on the shield together. My task was to paint it.

The design—which featured a red phoenix and the golden triangles of the Triforce—came out lopsided, skewed: definitely a ninth-grade amateur's first effort.

"One test left," Pop-Pop said, after the paint had cured. Pop-Pop carried his oxygen tank up the hill behind the house; I held the shield by its straps, along with a Nerf pistol. We hiked well into the woods, ate blackberries off the branch, chatted about woodworking and patience, about the serious play of creating with bladed tools. And then, as the afternoon dimmed under the canopy of the trees, Pop-Pop leveled the Nerf pistol, and said, "If you want to play the hero, you'll need to learn to use the shield."

I picked up a gnarled stick, one twice the length of my arm, and then raised the shield. Like Link—just like Link. I braced myself, balanced my weight on my soles. The soft earth shifted. I readied the shield.

* * *

Perhaps I will share the poem inspired by the shack on Wopsy. After all, it's the closest I got to my own form of *Zelda*'s Spectacle Rock:

Find me a poet who is not mold teeming into arsenical
brilliance on the rotting struts of some cabin abandoned

in the thick of the spruce groves on forgotten Wopsononock
Mountain. Find me a poet who does not exhale an ecosystem of

microbial phonemes that coalesce into colonies of language
that multiply and mutate beyond the porch railing of their

speaker's intents. Find me a poet who does not press their
hand against the struts, the exposed rafters, the bowing

floorboards to test how each plank and timber resigns
itself to the tussle between play and decay. Find me a

poet who is not the boards sagging from the weight of
deer idly pacing the cabin's single room; find me a poet

who is not the crush of the deer's molars on the lichens
ripped from the mortar on the wall, or the gumming of

the deer's wet lips on the mottled, inscrutable photo
plate that remains mounted to the wall. Find me a poet

who does not keen to this like the steel wheels of the
freight trains squealing on the rusted tracks that corkscrew

up Wopsononock.

There is no trace of *Zelda* here, but I like to hope that the same sense of mystery, the same thrill of discovery, haunts it.

*

We weren't alone in calling the starter sword in *The Legend of Zelda* the "wooden sword." For every child playing *Zelda* that green-handled, brown blade was a digital prop—a cardboard cutout of a sword made from glued-together layers of cardboard, a clumsy sword-shaped thing sawed from a sheet of plyboard.

Decades later, Nintendo acknowledged this: Link's first sword was a wooden plaything, like Miyamoto's stick in the forests of Sonobe or my own in the woods behind my grandparents' house in Big Run. When Nintendo released *Hyrule Warriors* in 2014 for the Wii U, the pixel-art starter sword from *The Legend of Zelda* re-appeared as a comically overpowered hidden weapon, called exactly that: the "Wooden Sword."

* * *

Half a continent away, at the edge of the Red River of the North, I google Zerns. It's 2021; the COVID pandemic still rages. I'm in my fourth year as a faculty member at the University of North Dakota, where I teach creative writing and publishing courses. My classes are entirely online, to maintain social distancing and protect my students, myself, our community. When I'm not reading or prepping a surfeit of online content for my courses' Blackboard pages, I'm returning to the pixelated landscapes of my favorite Nintendo games—*Super Mario World*, *The Legend of Zelda* and its sequels, the *Fire Emblem* games on the Nintendo 3DS handheld. I'm expanding my game library; a significant chunk of my collection first came from Zerns, so I consider ordering from their vendors—if I can.

The Google results list the webpage, but on the right side of the page, a red bar tops the inset with the Wikipedia blurb and the address in Gilbertsville. "Permanently closed," reads the text in the red bar. The website remains active, but its last update is from 2017.

I call Joe, who's now living in Savannah. When he answers, I say, "Joe, Zerns."

"What?"

"They're closed. Permanently."

"Shit," Joe says. In the background, something sizzles, crackles. He's probably at work, salmon flanks and steaks searing at his elbow, the air a tangy mélange of fat and herbs and heat. I've shadowed him in kitchens before, studied him in the heat that hazes from the flattop, observed how with knives and scrapers he conducts protein and veg and spices from ingredients to orchestrated dish. "I got most of my photography stuff there."

"I know."

Joe cusses a while longer: his fucking Canon 35mm, dozens of lenses that would be impossible to replace, a camera bag that contained an infantryman's patches from the Korean war, a pocketknife with a hilt carved from an antler, and all that good fucking potato salad—the savory stuff, not the stuff that looks like pigeon shit.

I say, "But I still have that copy of *Ocarina of Time* you got there."

"You're shitting me. I was going to throw that fucker in the Susquehanna."

"And you almost did," I say.

* * *

Over a year later, I return to Pennsylvania: a pair of flights from Grand Forks to National Airport in Arlington, a long drive from the rental car kiosk in Union Station through the peaks and vales of the Appalachians through Maryland, and then into southern Pennsylvania. On I-99, I have to force my eyes to remain on the road: parallel to me, across a vast gulf dozens of miles wide, the Horseshoe Curve bends on the forge-hot red-and-orange of the autumn colors. Fall melting the summer into slag, until the trees and their bark are the iron-dead grey of winter.

I have not seen my grandmother since the fall of 2016, shortly after Pennsylvania went scarlet on the Electoral College map, kicking the election to Donald Trump. On that drive into Pennsylvania, I stopped at the Barnes & Noble in Altoona and bought a copy of Hillary Clinton's *Living History* and swore this was it, I was gone, I was done. I detoured into Bellwood to rescue the commendation that Obama had signed in recognition of my grandfather's military service from a literal stack of trash destined for the burn barrel. After that, I blazed up PA-865, en route to Grandma.

This time, though, I careen through Altoona and only stop for coffee and donuts at the Dunkin just off PA-36. No books, nothing else: I'm driving through morning fog and lost time.

And then I'm veering the rental car through Big Run and the wheels are scissoring along the chip-and-tar side streets; I hook the car into Grandma's driveway and slow up the hill, a path that always reminded me of the hidden, rural entrance to Adam West's Batcave. When I brake, Grandma already leans in the doorframe at the back of the house. Pop-Pop's replica canon is gone, only a darker swath of grey on the porch slab as a testament to where it once stood. And now there's a ramp from the screen door down to the porch, a sign of what I have missed. But it's still the porch where, thirty-two years ago, I received that first copy of *Zelda* under the remote stare of a fox.

By way of greeting, Grandma says, "I saw one of the foxes back on the hill this morning. They don't come out that often, anymore."

We go inside and talk for hours—about the noise that once filled her house, of grandchildren shouting out status updates on video games from different rooms, of the deer that grazed behind her house, of the games she designed for us. And the woods, too, were there: dangerous and close, lonely and alone, bristling with joyous unknowns.

ALISON CONDIE JAENICKE

What Are You Famous For?

ONE: Nobody

"I didn't do shit with my life."

My grandmother uttered these words contemplatively, sitting beside a window with sweeping Blue Ridge views, in a tan velvet wingback chair, her hair short copper, body small and sinking. We had gathered for Thanksgiving at my parents' house in Virginia's Shenandoah Valley, the house they had built for their retirement years, with land enough for all the fruits and vegetables, trees and shrubs they'd always dreamed of growing. Extended family clustered in various rooms while my mom toiled in the kitchen. My mother's signature holiday was Thanksgiving. She had hosted a family gathering almost every one of her fifty married years, and while she accepted some help, mainly she handled it all. In a room above us, cheers erupted from the men and a few women watching a football game on the massive flat screen. The few of us in the living room listened to my sister-in-law tell about the gift shop and gift basket business she had recently gotten off the ground, when suddenly, my grandmother's forehead wrinkled, and her eyes closed.

"What is it, Dee Dee?" I asked.

"I'm just sitting here thinking. Boy, what amazing things all you young people are doing." She shook her head gently. "But me? I didn't do shit with my life."

A wave of exclamation swelled up, and she raised her hand against it. "I'm not looking for sympathy. I've had a good, long life. But ninety years, and what did I do?"

She didn't know precisely when, but Dee Dee supposed and accepted she would die within a decade. She knew she would become disembodied like her dozen or so siblings before her, but she didn't know if she'd pass the century mark like her sister Katie, or go in her mid-nineties like her sister Margy. None of us knew cancer would take her in just a few years. When she turned eighty, she had told me she wasn't scared of death, only curious. Her declaration that she saw her life as meaningless alarmed me.

Emily Dickinson's lines echoed in my head: *"I'm Nobody! Who are you? / Are you—Nobody—too?"* Emily made it sound like a badge of honor, but I did not want to imagine my grandmother as a nobody, did not want to imagine a world without my grandmother's body in it. To me, the two of us were linked for all time. I had come into the world as her first grandchild on her fifty-first birthday, had lived in her house my first year, joining a household in Herminie, Pennsylvania, that included her three school-aged children, a husband, a mother-in-law, and my mother. She had fed and cared for me while my mother finished her student teaching. I transformed her exasperated expression—"Lordy"—into my label for her: Dee Dee.

"What do you mean you didn't do shit with your life!?" Everyone tumbled over themselves to praise her amazing afghans, her flaming Christmas pudding, her homemade chocolate confections. She stopped us. "Don't pay any attention to this old lady crying in her drink. I'm just an old crank." And with that she put her hands on the chair's arms and rose. "Let's see what's happening with the turkey."

TWO: Polka Hall of Fame

Growing up, I loved weekend days when my dad would put on an LP, dance around the rec room with invisible mic held near his singing mouth, and motion us kids to dance with him. When my mom started up the vacuum in another room, he'd turn up the stereo and sing louder. Ike and Tina Turner, Ray Charles, Blood Sweat & Tears, Gladys Knight & The Pips, Santana, the Beatles—albums by these groups were the ones we all loved from our family record collection. One album in the collection divided us: *Slovenian Polka Star Records Presents: Polkas That Made Yukon Famous*, recorded in 1973 by the Joe Grkman Orchestra. Our parents cherished it; we three kids loved to mock its ridiculous title, its gaudy orange cover featuring a black-and-white photo of an "orchestra" composed of five awkwardly coiffed white guys, two holding accordions, all smiling wildly about their little coal patch town, located across

Sewickley Creek from the Magee Mine in Yukon, Pennsylvania, a town now made famous by none other than themselves. The back of the album offered a photo of Joe Grkman, Jr., with long sideburns and fat tie, his Slovene buttonbox fanned out in front of him.

The Joe Grkman Orchestra "has been pleasing audiences with their special blend of Slovenian/Cleveland style of polkas and waltzes across the U.S. and abroad since their formation in 1967." So proclaims the Grkmania.com website. Three generations have now played in the band. They've won many awards and have been inducted into the American Slovenian Polka Foundation Hall of Fame. Joe Grkman Sr.—the band's leader until his death in 2014—earned a National Cleveland Style Polka Hall of Fame Lifetime Achievement Award.

My family especially prizes the band's Slovenian polkas. My dad is half Slovenian, and the Western Pennsylvania towns where my parents grew up, met, and married, are studded with Slovenians, whose smoked kielbasa, potica, and *halupkis* perfume most homes. Down the hill from my maternal grandparents' house in Herminie is a hall that once was the social center of town: the Slovene National Benefit Society (SNPJ) Lodge 87, chartered in 1908 and named *Prostomislci* ("Free Thinkers"), part of the national organization founded in Chicago just four years earlier. The Herminie SNPJ organization still exists, but the hall has become "The Crystal Ballroom Wedding and Event Center," a drop-ceilinged, chandeliered space where people can still sweep across the wooden floor to a good polka or a line dance or a melting pot of modern music.

When we were kids, we thought the album title *Polkas That Made Yukon Famous* laughable, but by the time I got married in 1991, I had come to love polkas, even borrowed the album for a time. (Now my dad reports he's given it to my Uncle Anthony, who built a house on family land in Herminie, and whose in-laws were from nearby, now-famous Yukon.) I loved polkas so ferociously that I recorded one of the album's jauntiest songs—"Triglav Polka"—for our wedding mixtape, placed it right next to a Los Lobos polka so dancers could keep up the spinning happy energy for two songs in a row. The tape was to be played on the band's breaks, a band with lead singer Stoney Bourke (my Uncle Michael's friend and former bandmate), in a newly configured wedding band called "The Biscaynes and the Hurricane Horns." We celebrated our marriage in the University of Maryland ballroom, on the campus where my dad earned his football fame. When "Triglav Polka" played, spinning couples filled the dance floor, some male-female, but many women pairs as well. I may have danced with my new husband or with my sister. Either way, my "yips" punctuating the song's high points were loudest of all.

THREE: Gridiron Records

In a small town like Herminie, fame comes by various routes, opportunities to latch onto it are greater than they are in a big city, and the fame lasts longer than the fifteen minutes claimed by Andy Warhol, a Pittsburgh boy, who went off and formed this philosophy in the Big Apple. Andy Warhol said: "More than anything people just want stars." (When my mother was born in Herminie in 1940, though, Warhol was thirteen, living nearby in Pittsburgh's Oakland neighborhood, his name still Andrew Warhola, son of Slovakian immigrants Ondrej Warhola, a construction worker, and Julia Warhola, an embroiderer.)

Almost twenty years ago, when my grandmother Dee Dee was still alive, but my grandfather Dut had passed, newly situated in Pennsylvania myself after years living in DC and then Tennessee, I traveled to a big picnic at my Uncle Anthony's house up the hill from my grandparents' home in Herminie. My uncle built his family's house near the apple orchard Dut and his brothers planted and tended, on land my grandparents gave Uncle Anthony when he returned from DC to raise his family in his hometown. He has land and a view of green rolling hills, Gobbler's Knob across the way, houses laid out on a grid spreading toward Main Street.

The party assembled lots of guests who had lived in the town their whole lives. Some clustered around the keg near the open garage door. Some looked through the plasticized pages in the three-ring binder of the soon-to-begin karaoke outfit—Kitchen Man and Dan—deciding which songs to request. Some admired my uncle's garden plot with tomatoes, peppers, basil, onions, and marigolds—the garden of a man who married an Italian, a man whose father grew bushels of tomatoes, gallons of strawberries, truckloads of melons. Whose father also planted an apple orchard with the idea of starting a business with his brothers but who was left holding the bill and the work of the harvest each fall.

I was throwing a football on the sloping lawn, maybe with a cousin, maybe my husband, and someone nearby, cup of beer in hand, commented to a friend: "Look at that girl throw."

And the friend said, “Well, you know who that is—that’s Dennie Condie’s daughter.” Raising his voice, he directed his question to me: “Ain’t you Dennie Condie’s daughter?” I smiled and nodded, threw the ball again, best spiral I could form, remembering my dad’s instructions to start with fingers on laces, follow through cleanly and fully, feeling pleasure as I watched its perfect rotation and arc.

At that moment, I was in my thirties, and so it had been over thirty years since my dad had starred on the Sewickley Bison football team, on the field I could see below me, kitty-corner from my grandparents’ house, and right across from what’s now a gas station/Dairy Queen. Thirty years plus, and they were still able to recall his feats and fame, fame I’ve heard about my whole life, and knowing it, even without seeing it, somehow made me feel special and powerful, like I had permanent gold dust coating my hands after handling the trophy.

A few years before the picnic, near the end of the wedding reception of my Uncle Anthony’s oldest daughter, Mary, after everyone had drunk quite a few, I discovered my dad at the bar in the middle of a circle of older guys. They were recounting specific plays in specific games from the late 1950s. Something like this: “Remember that one against Greensburg, your senior year, when all the scouts were in the stands, and you caught the ball on the kickoff, faced a pack of ’em on the right, juked to the left, leaped over a tackler, took it all the way back for a TD and left ’em all shitting in their trousers at the other end?” Nodding heads.

At University of Maryland, where they called him both “Dennis the Menace” and “The Flea,” my dad still has two records on the books (both ties with other players, one shared with a teammate): 1) Season Kickoff Returns for TD—Dennis Condie (Jr.), 1960—2 returns for season, and 2) Longest Kickoff return for TD—100 yards—Dick Novak/Dennis Condie vs. Virginia, 1960 (Novak returned to the 9-yard line, then lateraled to Condie who returned 91 yds. For TD.)

This is one sort of fame.

FOUR: Big Bands

My grandfather, Anthony Wilps, (better known throughout his adult life as “Shack,” but who I called Dut, and as the first grandchild, my nickname stuck) played drums and sang in big bands throughout the 1930s and 40s. On my walls hang framed sepia-tinted black-and-white photos of him in traditional tux and black bow tie, hair slicked back, smile suave, holding drumsticks behind the drum kit, bass drum painted with a lake scene. Throughout the years, his various bands were configured in different ways with different personnel—Leo Zornik & his Orchestra and Martin Serro Band were only two. (Incidentally, Herminie SNPJ records tell us that Anton Zornick was the lodge's first president, and "when Martin Serro reigned as President, c. 1970, the lodge drew its largest number of members.") No matter the bandleader's name, often the bands featured Shack Wilps on drums and Patty Bourke on clarinet and sax.

Recently, Patty Bourke's son Jook made an album featuring my Uncle Michael on drums—two musicians' sons who played together on and off since the late 60s. Jook dedicated the album to Patty and Shack and two musical families. The CD case features as background one of Patty and Shack's old bands in faded black-and-white, my grandfather's face imprinted on the cover again and again in copy after copy—a fame of sorts spreading through the world decades after his death. Superimposed is a color photo of the three current members: Jook Bourke (son of Patty, brother of Stoney), my Uncle Michael Wilps, with Ron Grkman on bass, standing in the Palace Lunch on Main Street, Herminie.

I grew up with these photos and stories of the bands. Before they were married, my grandmother Dee Dee's dance card filled up while Dut played the drums, giving a stern shake of the head when she danced with someone he didn't appreciate. I grew up knowing that as Dee Dee lay in her sister Margy's bed on Church Street in Herminie, giving birth to my mother in late December 1940, my grandfather was playing in a band to earn enough money to pay the doctor, the Herminie mine of the Ocean Coal Company having closed a few years before in 1937, leaving the men in town to scramble for whatever work they could find.

FIVE: Modesty is a Virtue

If my mother is famous for anything in this town, it's for being smart enough to get out, for being the first in her nuclear family to finish high school, the first to take herself off to college on her own dime, the first to follow her high school sweetheart to Maryland after his college football career transplanted him there, the first to pursue a career and raise a family away from those who raised her. If my mother is famous for anything in Herminie, no one talks about it; they don't shout it out on the hilltop, across the lawn, as they throw a football at my uncle's picnic.

My mom rejects the spotlight, gets angry if we talk about her high school years, look at pictures of her—she once grabbed away from my brother a photo of herself in a satin and chiffon prom gown sewn by Dee Dee. She threatened to burn the photo. Maybe she's burned it by now. Maybe she just hid it, feeling like it's nobody's business but hers and my dad's to see and reminisce over that time. Her stories of life before me are her stories, ones she seldom shares.

Once when she heard I was trying to cook up a small gathering for their fiftieth wedding anniversary, my mother called me to say: Don't. Don't do anything for us. I don't want people looking at us, standing up and saying we did anything special. We didn't. What's so special about sticking together for fifty years?

I read between the lines: sticking together equates with inertia, not action or achievement. It's what's expected of any married couple, and meeting expectations is nothing to throw a party for. And yet, starting from a point of pennilessness, they achieved so much together: raised three kids and put us through college, bought and sold three houses (including a vacation home on a lake), taught and coached and led and earned and saved and traveled and built a beautiful life together worth celebrating.

Once she rebuffed me on the topic of their golden anniversary, she moved on to her funeral. While we're on the subject of standing up and saying something about me, she said, I don't want you to do it when I die, either. There's nothing to say about my life. I lived, I didn't do anything notable, I died.

I started to protest, remind her about all she'd achieved. Her career teaching math, raising three responsible kids. What about that Virginia Volunteer of the Year Award you received in Richmond a few years back? All your work at church and for the women in the shelter? But she stopped me. I've said it. Let's move on. Nothing to see here.

(And what would she think of the snapshot I'm offering here? The light I'm shining on this moment when she's asked me to spotlight nothing of her? Choosing this moment and image above any other I might have captured—images of her generosity, creativity, energy: planting, picking, and canning strawberries, tomatoes, peppers, or cucumbers, for instance, or making clothes, quilts, curtains, or slipcovers. Is it a daughter's betrayal or duty to tell the fullest family story she can? Maybe it's both.)

Emily Dickinson's poem "I'm Nobody! Who are you? (260)" ends this way: "*How dreary—to be—Somebody! / How public—like a Frog— / To tell one's name—the livelong June— / To an admiring Bog!*" Emily herself might have been mortified to see the publicity and limelight she now receives, the way her words have traveled so far beyond her hometown bog.

SIX: War Hero

While my mom refuses the notion she has a legacy worthy of recognition and is utterly unsentimental about her own place in the world, she constantly feeds me family stories to digest, hold, pass on. She frequently reminds me of all the ways others in the family are famous. Look at them, she says, not me.

Her dad's older brother Ralph Wilps left the coal mines to play football at Pitt and is still listed in the school's official media guide as a Panthers letterman from 1926–29. Two other brothers—Mike and Will Wilps—went off to fight in Northern Africa during WWII, and my mom "wrote" letters to Will before she could form letters of the alphabet, crayoned scribbles on page after page. Will later became famous for the way he died: burned to death at age 85 on a hillside near his home, just below my Uncle Anthony's, as he attended to the weekly garbage burn.

Most famous was her cousin Tony Herbert, who left Herminie to enlist in the Army during WWII, was turned away because he was only fourteen, then went on to become "the most decorated enlisted man of the Korean War," according to the blurb on his book *Soldier,* a book my mom has kept on her bookshelf for decades. A United States Army officer who served in both the Korean and Vietnam Wars and reached the rank of lieutenant colonel, he reported witnessing war crimes in Vietnam, including serial executions of detainees and water torture of a prisoner. When his commanding officer refused to investigate and the Army relieved him of his command, he continued to serve but went on to write several books about his experiences, most notably *Soldier*, in which he details his war crimes allegations. He appeared on *The Dick Cavett Show*, was challenged by Mike Wallace on *60 Minutes*, and filed lawsuits against the Army and CBS, which lingered in courts for much of the rest of his life. He was eager to serve, performed extraordinarily, witnessed atrocity, and was not believed. He was famous for speaking out, but he was not believed because like most sons of coal towns, he was expected to serve and not question those in power.

My first cousin once removed, Anthony Bernard Herbert was born on April 17, 1930, in Herminie, to Charles Herbert, a coal miner, and the former Mary Theibert, one of my grandmother Dee Dee's older sisters. I recall visiting Aunt Mary's house in Herminie when I was little, how the kitchen overflowed with kids, stuff, chaos. She opened the bottom drawer of her oven—in most homes filled with skillets and pans—to reveal a cache of toys, and I happily sat on the floor playing while the women sat at the table and caught up over cups of coffee.

SEVEN: The Milliner and Her Daughters

My grandmother's maiden name was Irene Lucy Theibert; she took the confirmation name Cecilia in the Catholic Church as a teenager and then the last name Wilps when she married in 1937. Born January 14, 1911, she was the last of eleven children (or thirteen, depending which records you believe) born to Harriet Bayley Theibert and Jules Nicholas Theibert, son of a French glassmaker who somehow made his way to West Bromwich, England. Jules and his English bride Harriet were married in the Anglican Church, had a few kids, brought them to New Kensington, Pennsylvania, then had a few more, including Katie and Margy, who I came to know well. The Theiberts lost some in childbirth, lost two young daughters to tuberculosis. When the doctor said it wasn't safe to raise a family along the foggy and polluted Allegheny River, they moved out to "the country" in Herminie, closed down one store, opened another.

About her mother, Dee Dee said:

> Mum was a milliner, always making hats, sewing for people. We had a store, and Katie and Margy were always working at the store. One side of the store was ice cream, a candy

> case, a case with ribbons. Everybody just waited to see the Christmas window. Mum used to make things that looked like air balloons, hanging. Fancy crocheted lace. My mother could do anything. Lunchtime she'd make creamed shrimp on toast. Fancy dishes. Margy, too. She could always whip up something. Salads—she made salads so beautiful.
>
> Mum was busy all the time. Holidays, for Easter, she was busy making hats. So who took care of me? Nobody, really. That's true. Nobody did. I can't remember my childhood in that house. Mum was busy. Margy and Katie were busy. Johnny and I did whatever we wanted. My neighbor friend—whose family owned the hotel—we used to play every day. That's where I ate most of the time. I never remember eating at home at all, really, when I was a child.

I can't account for Dee Dee's contradictory recollections about her mother's cooking. She was in her right mind, sharp all the way until the end. But who can say what becomes of memories after more than eighty years stewing in the brain?

Andy Warhol's mother, born Júlia Justína Zavacká, was herself an embroiderer and artist. Her decorative handwriting accompanied Andy's illustrations, and she won awards for her lettering, including one from the American Institute for Graphic Arts. In 1957, she illustrated a small book called *Holy Cats.* You can read all about her, see her artwork, if you visit The Andy Warhol Museum in Pittsburgh, just down the Allegheny River from where my great-grandmother had her first store.

Near the end of her life, my grandmother had collected the flotsam of many years of women's work crocheting, tatting, embroidering, beading, sewing. On one of my last visits to her house, when she was the only one left and lived alone, she took me to an upstairs bedroom and opened all the drawers in a dresser, revealing a stash of handmade goods. "Take what you want," she said. "I don't know what to do with it all!"

Family lore tells me my great-grandmother Harriet Theibert, milliner and business owner, was better known than her husband Jules, who supposedly invented a miner's helmet with electric headlight, to replace the dangerous ones with flames, but he never patented it. I have in my house Harriet's handiwork, but I don't have Jules' helmet. The tatting and embroidery embodies her artistic work.

The milliner kept a storefront on Main Street in Herminie and was known for her hats in the window. After the store was gone, she still crocheted and sold layettes for newborns. Her daughter Katie was known for having her own storefront of sorts, as postmaster of Herminie for nearly thirty years, a title and role she took on after her husband's death in a coal mining accident. She was known for living to age 103. Her obituary talked about her job as well as her family, including her one son. The milliner's daughter Margy lived her life in Herminie, too, but when she died, her obituary could claim for her no storefront, no job title, no children.

My grandmother Dee Dee's obituary titled her "homemaker," told of her four children and extended family relations. The last of her siblings to leave, she was left holding the bag of mixed goods.

I took from Dee Dee some but not all of the linens and ladies' hankies, tablecloths and doilies, veils and shawls. When she passed these on to me, she no longer knew whose handiwork was whose, but she did press into my palms a blood-red beaded bag crocheted by my artistic and childless Great Aunt Margy, twelve years her senior. She passed on to my mother who then passed on to me: yards of handmade lace that if stretched out would reach the length of a football field, endzone to endzone. My mother washed and ironed it carefully and wound it up, stored it in clear plastic bags. I keep it in our guest room, in a drawer of Aunt Margy's bedroom furniture, bought for her wedding in 1922, the same day in July as my own wedding. The wood of the furniture is dark as swamp water.

What do I do with this heavy legacy, this large glory box? I have a daughter, Margaret, named for my Aunt Margy, who never got the children she wanted. Our daughter is as artistic as her female forebears, if not more so. But will my Margaret be able to carry all that the milliner and her daughters left behind? Can I?

EIGHT: Hail Mary

In football terms, when a quarterback throws a "Hail Mary," it is an act of desperation, a long pass with little chance of succeeding. The term comes from the Catholic prayer to the Holy Mother: "Hail, Mary, full of grace, the Lord is with thee. Blessed art thou among women, and blessed is the fruit of thy womb, Jesus. Holy Mary, mother of God, pray for us sinners, now and at the hour of our death." Help us. Give us strength.

After I left the Catholic Church, it's Mary I missed. Why such love and veneration for this long-suffering mother, known for her submission, her bowed head, her womb? Why do I miss her so much? Who wants to be known for obedience and sorry? I have no more practical use for Mary Mother of God than I do for a football field's length of lace. And yet I keep them both.

I wonder whether nostalgia clouds my desires and impulses. Nostalgia for a former coal town I never really lived in, for a time I never lived in, for a religion that still makes women subservient to men.

Sometimes I put in earbuds and listen repeatedly to one of my favorite songs until tears flood me. In "Mary," Patty Griffin sings plaintively: "Mary you're covered in roses, you're covered in ashes / You're covered in rain / You're covered in babies, you're covered in slashes / You're covered in wilderness, you're covered in stains /. . . Jesus said Mother I couldn't stay another day longer / Flies right by and leaves a kiss upon her face / While the angels are singin' his praises in a blaze of glory /Mary stays behind and starts cleaning up the place."

As I listen, I think of Dee Dee, how she cleaned other people's houses to earn enough money to make ends meet: cleaned for a family with young kids who gave me hand-me-down clothes, cleaned the nearby home of her own older sister Katie, who had money to spare from her long stint as Herminie's postmaster. I think of Dee Dee's sister Mary, raising so many sons who went off to war. I think of my great-grandmother Mary Wilps, Dut's mother, Lithuanian immigrant who raised nine children after her coalminer husband died of the Great Influenza epidemic in 1919.

I think, too, of the Biblical story of Martha and Mary. When Jesus visited the two sisters, it was Mary who sat and listened to his lessons and stories, sat in contemplation, while Martha rushed around cooking and cleaning.

There are many ways to be a Mary.

In the mid-1800s, Mary Harris Jones (aka Mother Jones), Irish immigrant trained as a dressmaker and teacher, met and married a skilled iron molder and staunch unionist in Memphis, Tennessee, had four children with him, then lost both husband and all their children to a yellow fever epidemic in 1867. After returning to Chicago and commercial dressmaking, she opened her own shop, grew disenchanted with the divide between the wealthy Chicago families she sewed for and the jobless and hungry folks she saw on the streets. After losing her shop in the Great Chicago Fire of 1871, she spent the rest of her life moving around the country, agitating for workers' rights.

When I listen to the song "Mary" and think of all the Western Pennsylvania Marys in my family, I think of Mary (Mother) Jones' appearance at age 73 at the Westmoreland County Coal Strike of 1910-11 (also known as the Slovak Strike because about 70 percent of the miners were Slovak immigrants.) When miners' wives were arrested in the summer of 1910 for harassing strikebreakers and company security personnel, then jailed with their babies and small children, Mother Jones encouraged the women to sing to their children in jail continuously (she'd bring them milk and fruit, she said), and the singing kept the people of Greensburg awake for five nights straight and ultimately led to the women's release.

When my grandmother declared that she "didn't do shit" with her life, I felt compelled to write her a letter. I told her how she shaped me by teaching me to crochet and bead, by saving up and giving me Christmas Club money each year so I could buy gifts for others, by making us all strawberry jam and stewed tomatoes and peach preserves so we never had to eat store-bought, by writing me letters, by sharing a birthday with me, by taking care of me in her home for the first year of my life. I wanted to tell her she had lived a life that would not be cut off by death.

I sent the letter to her then, near the turn of the twenty-first century, but even now, long after her death, I am still writing the letter. I don't think I'll ever be done. The Book of Ecclesiasticus (44:1) declares: "Let us now praise famous men, and our fathers that begat us." These words I write now are part of that endless letter, unspooling still. Let us Now Praise Famous Women. I praise my grandmother and all the other women who begat me. Maybe what Dee Dee wanted was not praise or fame. Maybe, like my mother, she did not need anyone to celebrate her life. What did she want? I try to get inside her mind and cannot. I can only know what I want for her and for all the Marys: to know their worth. To know the many meaningful ways to be a Mary.

RACHEL KESSELMAN

When Are You Coming Back?

My mother had hung the autumn leaf decals from my childhood in her new kitchen window. As I peered out over the sink, their bright oranges and yellows blocked out the more muted colors of the mountains in the distance. This window was the only one in the house that you could see out of; the sills of all the others held shutters that covered the bottom halves of the glass, while the top panes were shaded by outdoor awnings.

"It's so dark in here," I said.

"I like the natural light," my mother said.

I had arrived in Pennsylvania two days earlier for a friend's wedding, myself newly engaged. Already I had found the Wyoming Valley unchanged: backroads held the same potholes, overhead power cables drew large black lines over the trees, and houses made no sound. The Susquehanna, snaking its way around the mountains, still appeared sleepy despite its legacy of destruction. Whenever I came back, I experienced the unsettling sensation of both finding and losing myself, comforted by the permanence of this place that was my home, terrified by its stagnancy. I would visit for another few days before returning to Paris, where I'd been living for a decade.

"Show me your ring," my mother said.

I held out my hand, and she examined it, moving my finger in different directions to see the light in the diamond.

"I guess you really aren't going to come back, then?"

"I didn't plan to live so far away," I said. "The divorce made things hard."

"It was harder for me."

Mom resumed looking at the television. I looked back through the leaves stuck on the window. My father lived on the other side of the mountain in the house he had built for us when I was twelve.

"Your grandfather is waiting for us," Mom said. "Let's go."

The tree at the end of the driveway got sick and died. Grandpa had it removed a few years ago, leaving a wide-open view of his small white house and the blue Virgin Mary shrine next to the porch. The rosebush that used to grow haphazardly behind the statue was gone, too, uprooted and discarded after it started producing more brown leaves than buds.

As we pulled into the driveway, the dog howled from his coop, and I saw there was not one but two of them now, anxious beagles rubbing their snouts up against the chain link doors of their prisons. Grandpa raised his hands up like an air traffic controller as my mother put the car in park.

"I was waiting for yous!" he said. "I want to show you something."

We followed him into the living room. His eyes watered constantly; he wiped them with a blue handkerchief he kept in the pocket of his Dickies. Inside, he showed me the two-foot wedding portrait of my late grandmother propped up behind her ashes on the television. There were two photographs of graves wedged in the portrait's frame that he then removed.

"See this here, what does that say?"

I read his last name from the gravestone. Underneath it, an abbreviation of his first name was written with an expression of gratitude: *Thank's Ed.*

"That's right," he said. "I bought them eight plots down the cemetery ten years ago—two hundred a piece back then. Now they're so expensive you'd never get a deal like that today."

He held out the second photograph to me in his shaking hands.

"Now read that," he said.

I read my grandmother's maiden name, underneath which was her father's first name.

"That's right," he said. "Your grandmother said she wanted to go there, but she's still here." He pointed to the white box on the TV. "Now yous can wait until I go and then you can just do one day for the both of us. If you can make it, of course."

"Dad, when's the last time you took those dogs out for a walk?" my mother asked.

"Who does she look like?" my grandfather asked, pointing to my mother.

"My mom?"

"I know that's your mother. Who does she look like?"

He pointed to my grandmother's portrait.

"I know she ain't blonde, but she looks like her."

"Dad, the dogs," my mother said.

"You know that one dog goes real fast so I can't take him out no more."

My grandmother's pink imitation Tiffany lamp was still in the bay window, but instead of being surrounded by seasonal decorations, my grandfather had inserted a one-foot miner figurine carved entirely from anthracite and a miniature wagon of coal pulled by two black horses. My grandfather saw me looking at them.

"All my life I been lucky," he said. "My father come home one day from the mines real late and he didn't have no leg. Two mine cars crashed right into each other, and his leg was between them."

"She doesn't want to hear about that," my mother said.

"I had to work down there a little bit, but like I'm telling you I been lucky all my life. Went to the army and they put me over Alaska instead of Korea. And then I got the job out the prison, so I didn't have to go back down them mines. Your cousins work there now, too," he said. "You could go get a job out there and come back."

When we stepped outside the house, the air felt like it was from another universe, fresh and cool. My mother walked ahead of me to the dogs, yelling back without looking.

"We have to help them get out for at least a little bit," she said.

When she opened the coop, the dogs ran like bullets, circling the house around and around as though they were attached by an invisible string. Mom waited for them to tire out, and toward their sixth rotation they slowed down. We attached their leashes, and they pulled us up the driveway to the little creek that ran in front of the house.

Grandpa hollered after us. He was holding a piece of paper now, waving it from the front porch.

"Go see what he wants," Mom said. She took the dog leash I was holding. "I can't do it anymore."

As I approached, I understood that the paper was the church bulletin, a document I knew well from my Catholic upbringing.

"Now wait," he said, "I have to show you the most important part."

He pointed to the bottom of the second page, where there were four numbers: the budget for the church bazaar. One showed what the church raised last year compared to what they needed, and another what they raised this year compared to what they needed.

"They need more money!" he said. "People going to church on their computers now and they don't give no donations."

The dogs pulled Mom back towards the house. I took one leash back from her and we opened the coop, filled with hay and excrement. The dogs jumped back in without much struggle and resumed looking out at us from the wires.

"When are yous coming back?" Grandpa asked.

"We'll be back again before she leaves," my mother said.

As my mother backed out of the driveway, my grandfather stood in front of the garage, watching the car move as though it were a movie. When we got onto the road, Mom honked the horn, and he waved, never moving from his standing position.

At my mother's the next morning, I descended from the upstairs bedroom to the kitchen coffee pot.

"Uncle Henry died last night," my mother said, announcing her presence at the kitchen table. "Grandpa's brother. I don't think you ever met him."

I poured a cup and looked out again through the leaf decals of the kitchen window. Fall was one of the sunniest seasons here. Light poured over the mountain like paint.

"He fell down the stairs," she said. "Now they're thinking it might have been his girlfriend that pushed him. She just got out of jail for the second time."

"Jesus," I said.

"His wife died a few years ago. They never had kids, so they did well. He was a math teacher and she worked, too. Traveled a lot overseas. Germany and all that."

"Does Grandpa know?"

"I have to call him," she said. "That girlfriend wanted his money. You know when Grandma died Grandpa sold the car to Uncle Henry and he gave it to that girlfriend."

"How did a math teacher start dating a criminal?"

"They met at the gun show."

The TV was still on, filling the hole in our conversation.

"I thought we could go for a walk today," my mother said.

"I'm having lunch with Dad."

My mother called out to the cat. She waited a minute, then turned to me. "Tomorrow we'll go for a walk."

Every surface of Mom's house was covered in decor: pumpkins, candles, wooden signs, and snow globes. I cleared a space on the kitchen table for my coffee mug next to a floral cardboard box.

"That's stuff from Grandma," my mother said. She opened the box and started taking out pouches and boxes of jewelry. "Most of it's junk, but you could probably get some money for the gold."

As I peered down into the box, I discovered my mother's own pieces of jewelry, pre-divorce, mixed inside. A hand-written card from my father stuck out from underneath the grey and black velvet boxes that suddenly made me think of coffins.

"I should take a shower," I said.

"You can take a bath in my new tub if you want," Mom said. "Still paying that off. Ten thousand they charged me."

When I finished, my mother was waiting for me with a small brown box that had been duct taped at the bottom to stay together.

"If you're going to see your father, you could take this to him."

When I was growing up, my father worked in construction, always dreaming of becoming an architect. He finally finished his degree when I was in middle school, taking night classes after work, and once he was licensed, he started designing us a new house. My mother could not read blueprints, so Dad made several different foam board models of different houses. Our living room table turned into a miniature village of new futures, complete with tiny trees made from twigs my sister and I would find outside.

Inside my mother's brown box was one of these houses.

This particular model was dented and ripped, revealing some of the foam underneath the board like skin removed from a body. The roof over the garage was detached and turned upside down, revealing the text in the room underneath: "ATTIC SPACE." I could see the window I'd looked out of as a teenager, its measurements written in a tiny draftsman font.

Mom picked up the house with one hand to reveal what was sitting underneath: the wooden camels Dad had brought back from his trip to Jerusalem that used to sit on my parents' dresser. She let go of the house and it plopped back on top of the camels, the main roof beginning to detach from the impact.

"No," I said.

"I didn't think it was so much to ask to take a small box."

There was only one place I could see my father when I came in for a visit, a small sushi restaurant where most customers ordered take out. Dad lived alone in our house on the hill, occupying only the downstairs floor where he maintained a flood of blueprints, file folders, half-empty glasses, and cardboard boxes. It was better for both of us to see each other in public. On these occasions, his speaking voice was as loud as a scream, as though with one outing he'd had to make up for all the time he'd been in isolation.

As I drove to the restaurant, I received a call from him asking what time we were to meet. He explained he had fallen asleep and would be fifteen minutes late.

I sat in a booth. The restaurant was quiet. Upon arrival, Dad clapped his hands and yelled as soon as he saw me, as though the entire restaurant were ours. His white hair was combed back farther than I remembered, and he had put on weight, his neck attached to a mass of hard red skin. His glasses hid his fatigue, and it was only when he took them off to reattach one of the temples that I saw the bags under his eyes, puffy and wrinkled like raisins.

"I was up all night working on new drawings," he said. "They change one thing and don't realize then I have to redraw everything else to code."

He handed me a white envelope with my name written in all capital letters, in his draftsman handwriting, as though paying a toll.

Dad ordered what he always ordered: soup, salad, and a California roll he'd eat with a fork. He spoke of his dream of leaving everything behind to go to Texas, saying he'd looked at ranches he could afford where he'd have no neighbors, where he'd have nothing but a large plot of land.

The waitress came over to retrieve our plates, recognizing us from our many other visits to the restaurant.

"This is your daughter?" she asked.

"Yes, that's my daughter who lives in Paris."

"I have three. They don't want to have kids they say. I can understand it," she said. "I just hope they don't regret it later."

"They do their own thing," he said.

"I just don't know who will take care of them," she said. "They'll take care of me, but who will take care of them?"

"I never had parents," Dad said. "No one took care of me."

Outside the restaurant, Dad gave me a hug and asked when I was leaving. We made plans for another lunch, same time, same place, the day I'd be leaving.

"Love ya!" he yelled as he walked away.

Opening the envelope in the car, I found five perfectly flat one-hundred-dollar bills.

There were two old pictures of my mother on her refrigerator: one at a baptism where she was holding a baby and another with a friend on the beach from what looked like several decades ago. I asked who the people in the pictures were and if they had any relation.

"Oh, I don't know," she said. "I put those there to remind myself to lose weight. Look how thin I was!"

We were getting ready to go on our walk. My mother was putting on shoes she ordered online; she explained they were supposed to be top-of-the-line and waterproof, but she was disappointed with their quality.

"Another hundred dollars down the drain."

We made our way through the tiny street of tiny houses. Locals called these three blocks "Toy Town" as the houses appeared even tinier with the looming mountain in the background. Eventually, we approached the graveyard, twice the size of the development.

"I don't like walking back here," she said.

"I guess it's pretty depressing to walk through a cemetery."

"No," she said. "I don't think of it that way. They're resting. I just don't like walking on the pavement—the trail's up here."

American flags dotted the tombstones, microscopic in comparison to the ancient trees shading them around the cemetery. We walked until we approached a path with a sign that read "PRIVATE PROPERTY."

"I don't think I want to live until I'm ninety," Mom said, advancing down the path. "Another twenty years and I'm good."

We arrived at what appeared to be a pond. My mother explained it was one of the reservoirs for the Susquehanna, rising and falling with the rain. The piles of culm behind it made it look like we were on another planet, the gray ash-like hills like something I'd seen in a dinosaur movie as a child.

"I like to stand here, in the dead silence," she said. "Away from it all."

Just as she closed her eyes, though, her watch buzzed.

"We walked a mile!"

The path wound through abandoned railroad tracks, relics from a time when Wilkes-Barre was connected to the outside world to deliver coal. A mattress and toilet lay to the sides of the iron rods, tall grass pushing itself up out of the Earth in spite of the obstacles.

Eventually, we made it back out to an empty baseball diamond with two metal picnic tables. The grass here was high, too, and Mom said there was a problem with the ownership of the park. No one was responsible for it.

Back at the house, we sat in front of the TV. Mom was on her iPad, leaving me to the commercials for Medicare benefits and discount furniture. A heavily made-up woman appeared in front of a blank white screen, asking if we'd heard of Comcast's latest promotion. She then multiplied into ten and twenty identical women, illustrating the speed at which the Internet connection could bring new life.

I looked at my mother. I wanted to say I was sorry, a magic word that could shelter us like a blanket in the cold. I wanted my dad to be there. I wanted to have never left. I wanted everyone to come back to life.

LEONARD KRESS

Centralia Mine Fire

In Centralia, in the Appalachian Mountains of Northeastern Pennsylvania, there's no need to descend into the underworld, the realm of the dead, the realm of prophecy and hidden insight. Here, on what used to be a street lined with white aluminum-sided homes, edged lawns and wading pools, well-tuned and tended pickups—the underworld seeps up out of the ground, rising swirling and sulfurous from barely visible slits and fissures in the earth. The topsy-turvy displacement is almost complete. Charred roots tendril out from the ash and slag and gravel mounds that haven't yet spilled into the hot depressions. The mammoth anthracite coal seam that runs for twenty miles in either direction at a 57% angle has been burning for over sixty years now with no sign of letting up.

We've had to walk up into the hills, to reach this underworld; we've had to ascend in order to descend. We are all replicating the hero's journey, nervously excited kids included, though there is one man here already who seems more heroic than the rest of us. He's ripped a branch from a barkless dead limb and he's poking the ash, leading his family and other followers across a mound. Each time he pokes, prods, scratches the surface, sticks the ground, new fissures appear, until he's surrounded by stanchions of smoke like a stage Mephistopheles or a rock star in concert or a shaman in his lodge.

"They'll tell you it was spontaneous combustion that's the official version," he says, "but I know that's not the truth." Fresh new streams of sulfurous gases swirl in the wind and dissipate. Steadier streams shoot up all around us. "I grew up here," he continues, "lived here till the late sixties—left to fight in Vietnam. For years everyone would dump their trash down this mineshaft. It was like one big god-damned fuse—and there was this huge keg party going on and this guy had to go to work and didn't want his girlfriend hanging round—so he started the fire. I know it's true cause it was my brother-in-law from over in Mount Carmel. Though he won't admit it now."

Mike's his name, last name an indefinable glomeration of Ukrainian, Polish, and Slovak clusters of consonants. He doesn't live far away, he explains, but this is the first time he's brought his family—wife and two teen-agers who've never seen him in this role before. Reading or Wilkes-Barre or Allentown—he's got his own business installing security alarms or basement waterproofing. I don't catch which, because I'm nervous that my own kids, in their search for pocket-size lumps of anthracite, will slip and slide down into a hidden shaft or that their sneaks will blaze up from the heat.

Mike points to the last remaining houses lower down the slope. Less than a dozen old folks who've known no other home than Centralia and refuse to know new ones. The mayor, official or not—no one seems to know whether the town's been officially disestablished or not, with an *I Love Centralia* sign on his front lawn. He's ninety-seven and the only male not in the throes of Black Lung. He ran a funeral home for decades, the mines provided him with a good livelihood, why should he leave? I scan the hills looking for the sun to send my way the golden glint from any remaining Byzantine church domes—there is only one parched blue onion across the valley. "The government's hands are tied till they leave or die," Mike says. He points to the Ukrainian Cemetery further up the hillside. "The fire left them all alone, mostly miners and their families, almost a miracle, you might say. Everything else for a mile around burned-out—those graves untouched." Of course, I think, they're already dead. Here in Centralia, where the underworld has risen to the surface, where all of us, guests, tourists, and guides alike, briefly celebrate its encroachment.

CLAIRE T. LAWRENCE

Bear

At night the forest around our house sings to us, my husband and I. Peepers mate by the pond. Crickets creak. Sometimes a pack of coyotes passes the house, their yowls and yips cacophonous and sudden. Owls echo through the trees. We sit in the living room and read each night, our light-bound space tucked into the deep, living dark. It is an island, away from the heaving and struggle of the human world, protected and lonely at once.

One of those singing nights we were sitting on the couch when the dogs started going sniff crazy along the bottom of the sliding glass doors to our deck. You can't see out there unless you turn on the light, so that's what Mike got up to do.

"Be careful, it's probably a bear," I said.

"I doubt it," he said. "My guess is racoon."

He flipped the switch and there he was, the king of all bears. At first, we couldn't quite tell what he was he was so big. Monster was what my brain said.

"Fuck!" Mike said and turned off the light again. "Huge bear!"

We've had bears on the porch before. But they were lady bears, like the one who broke into our bird feeder and cut her paw, leaving a trail of brownish blood smeared across the deck and down the stairs. She was maybe the size of a very big dog—170 pounds tops. This bear was 600 pounds if he was an ounce.

"Mike," I hissed, "Turn the light back on! I want to see him." The flicking of the lights had been enough to warn the bear and he turned away from the bird feeder he was crushing in his paws. I pressed myself against the glass.

I love bears. Up on Montour Ridge where we live, just west of the small town of Danville, black bears are native and pretty ubiquitous. During the worst part of the pandemic, when I was teaching online, I would have the students' sad, half-assed papers open on one of my screens and on the other one of the PA Department of Natural Resources' webcams which focused on a bear hibernating under someone's porch. That's it, just a cam with a bear sleeping. I watched her hulking form rise and fall for months, soothed by her snoring and soft grunts. Until one day. there were cubs, joyful cubs, growling for milk and then, when they were older, playing and waking their mother, who would swat them or cup them to her teats.

"No lights!" Mike hissed back at me and grabbed the dogs, neither of whom had figured out there was a massive invader yet. This was a good move on his part, because who knows what would have happened if the bear had heard us. The glass of the sliding door, while thick, would do nothing to stop a creature that size, especially if the dogs started barking. But mercifully they were quiet as the bear swung around to face us. A whiff of something deep and musky slid under the door as he looked at the glass where we stood, a reflected ghost couple, maybe a foot or two from his face. His back was so fat it made his head look tiny; he must have just woken up from his winter nap. This was bear incarnate, glossy, and sublime.

He sniffed the air. We stared, frozen.

Then he must have decided we weren't a threat because he turned again, slowly, and ambled down the porch stairs and right over a solid wrought iron fence, bending it into a gnarled version of itself.

"Shit," Mike said, after a few minutes of awed silence.

"Shit is right," I said. "I wish you'd kept the light on though."

"Don't be stupid," he said and locked the door, as if that would keep out a bear. He was shaking a little. "I think we should turn out the lights in here as well, just until we're sure he's gone."

But me, I wanted that bear to come back. I could have watched his dark bulk for hours, smelled his wild smell, let him wreck the porch. I would even have followed him back into the howling forest, drank its darkness like mother's milk. We'd been stuck indoors for almost two years. I didn't believe in safety anymore.

SHU-JIANG LU

The Sound of My Rural Home

In mid-March 2001, the second year into my teaching as an adjunct faculty at Virginia Commonwealth University in Richmond, I received the job offer from University of Pittsburgh at Greensburg, located in Westmoreland County in Western PA. I wrote to several of my professors in London, Ontario, with the news. One of them sent me a postcard, congratulating me first, then asked: Greensburg sounds rather rural, is it?

I took the word, *rural*, quite literally at the time. To me, it was just an adjective related to the countryside, such as Greensburg, as opposed to the word "urban" related to cities, such as London where I studied and Richmond where I was teaching. Every morning, shortly before six in the morning, I would board the city bus and ride for over forty minutes across almost the entire city to VCU, an urban university sat right in downtown Richmond. On that bus ride, I watched and listened to the city waking up to the predawn light and morning sun. Bicycles, motorcycles, and cars started rolling through the streets; the pedestrians began rushing on the sidewalks, with their coffee mugs in one hand and briefcases in the other or with backpacks. Alongside the bus, the sound of the hurrying footsteps, ringing bicycle-bells, and rumbling motorcycle and cars' engines surged, a tide of the bustling noise of the city.

That bustling noise of a city is what I have been used to and familiar with. Born and growing up in a city and living thereafter in one city after another, from my native home in China to my adopted homes in Canada and US, I always see myself as a city girl.

That is, until I came to Greensburg, where I have since become a country girl who has learned the new meaning of the word *rural* and who feels blessed with a rural home, the home that speaks to me through its rural sound—that of the heartbeat of the land and its people.

For most, if not all, of us, where we go and stay on this earth deeply affects how we think and inevitably shapes who we are. In his essay, "Narrative and Landscape," native American writer Barry Lopez describes two kinds of landscapes: one is external, the one we see—its plants, animals, weather, climate, and geology (78). The other is an interior landscape, the one that projects a part of the exterior landscape within us. What brings together these two landscapes—those of the land and human heart, Lopez contends, is storytelling. The stories, claims Lopez, such as that of a hunter confronting yet connecting with a wolverine—the story with which Lopez opens his essay (76)—energize him and renew his sense of purpose of life, leading him to a deeper understanding of the relations between the human and the natural worlds.

Living in Greensburg for over twenty years, I have heard many stories from this land. Each story has its own special sound—those of my child, the feathered and furry creatures, the train/tunnel whistle, and creek. Together, they speak to my heart in the language of my rural home—that of love, strength, and hope.

* * *

On a late-July weekend in 2001, four months after I accepted the offer from Pitt-Greensburg, my husband packed our dark purple Trooper and drove my three-year-old daughter and me out of the city of Richmond and—as he joked—headed to the countryside. By that late afternoon, we arrived at our first home in Greensburg, a two-bedroom apartment on the second floor of a three-story red brick building in Southwest Greensburg. The building sat at the foot of a hill-like street, overlooking Route 30 West. We could see through the open window cars flashing by but barely hear the sound of engines which must have been softened by the wooded hills and open fields around the building.

Two days later, my husband returned to Richmond for his work. It was just my girl and me—two "country girls" who would begin our careers as a preschooler and a teacher in a place surrounded by trees, fields, and hills of which we didn't take much notice at first as we were busy preparing for schools—hers and mine. My daily routine was to drive her to the daycare in the mornings before going to my school, to pick her up in the late afternoons, and to return to our apartment.

I did notice, however, with the dread of a rookie driver, that many streets in Greensburg are built on small and big hills. Driving on any of those streets feels to me like climbing mountains. Used to the flat and straight roads in Richmond, I was always nervous driving up and down those in Greensburg—especially when I had to stop at the traffic lights. With my foot firmly holding on the brake, I still couldn't help worrying that my car would roll back down the street with even a little slip.

The street in front of our building is much steeper than any others. Driving on that street each morning, first to my daughter's school and then mine, I was always tense. Luckily for me, I would make a right turn soon enough without having to drive all the way to the top, hidden mysteriously in the trees and bushes.

For my little girl, however, every turn away from the top was a turn away from a discovery and wonder.

Can we go all the way to the top, mama? Please? She would plead. I want to see what is out there, please?

Maybe next time, I said, not really meaning it. And never went, until that September day, the day that would change the world and every one of us.

Early that September morning, I went to school early and wondered, not knowing what was going on, why the campus was so quiet. No sooner had I sat down in my office than the phone rang. It was my husband who told me in a frantic tone about Flight 93 in Somerset County, which is only about forty miles away from Greensburg. Panic-stricken, I hurried to the preschool to pick up the girl and back to our apartment. For the rest of that morning, I held her tight in my arms as we watched the horrifying images on TV.

That evening she asked me if we could go out for a walk.

Feeling sad and suffocated staying inside the apartment all day, I also wanted to get out.

Where would you want to go? I asked her.

That hilltop, she answered. I want to go all the way to the top and see what is there.

Off we went, my right hand holding hers, climbing up the big hill, all the way to the top where, hidden in the tall trees, evergreens, and other bushes, we saw an elementary school building and its playground.

Before going to the playground, we stood on the top, hand in hand, for quite a while, looking down the hill, realizing how steep the road is and how high we had climbed.

From the hilltop where we were standing, where the trees and bushes grow thickly and deepen in green, we could see the winding road all the way to its bottom and beyond.

Beyond, we saw more trees and bushes, from which the lights from the houses and buildings sprinkled into the evening air like stars.

Beyond, we saw the open field with green grass and golden corn, waving gently in the sundown.

Beyond, we saw the orange and purple sky where the setting sun and rising moon met, forming a watery light floating back and forth, a mysterious and endless flow.

To see *beyond.*

That's what we needed and did at that time—to be able to go and to see beyond what we were stuck in—the sorrow and despair—to feel a renewed sense of hope and living.

That first time of climbing up that hill would be followed by many more.

It became our new routine to walk on that street every evening. On the way up, I would still hold my little girl's hand, but on the way down, I would carry her on my back as we ran down the hill, her arms wide open, flapping like a bird, screaming and laughing all the way until we reached the bottom and stopped in front of our building.

That hill, forever echoing the sound of my child's laughing, brings Greensburg closer to me as a home, where I would watch my girl grow, taking this home with her wherever she goes.

Into our third year in Greensburg, my husband found a job in a city called Columbia near the DC area, two hours closer to us. In July 2004, we packed up and hopped into our Trooper and headed to Columbia for the summer.

As we were driving away from Greensburg into the mountain on Route 30 East, what was unfolding before us was an enlarged picture of

Greensburg. On both sides of the road were rolling wooded hills, dense forests, vast grassland, corn and crop fields, dairy farms, farmland with cattle and horses, the red, blue, white, green houses, and the tall windmills with giant wheels slowly spiraling skyward.

Our girl could hardly stay still, her head glued to the window, looking out and shouting: look at that pretty house! Look at that cow! Look at those corns! Look at those windmills! The joy and excitement in her voice brought me back to that hilltop in Greensburg.

The thrill of climbing up and racing down that hill, though, became a hundred times stronger. With much bigger and steeper ups and downs on Route 30, the ride felt like an endless roller coaster. Each time we rode over one, my husband would raise his voice: roller coaster is coming! Another one! Ready! The girl would be as loud in returning: Yes ready Baba! Yah—! clapping while laughing.

To that laughter added music. The stereo would be playing—for that trip and many afterwards—"Take Me Home, Country Roads" by John Denver who was among the first American singers my husband and I got to hear in the mid-1980s while still in China. Riding through the hills on the country road in PA, we felt for the first time part of the song as we were part of the country road surrounded by hills, trees, farms, and fields.

Soon, the line, "take me home," would literally be sung or cried out by our daughter.

Early that evening, we arrived at my husband's one-bedroom apartment in downtown Columbia. Next day, after he went to work, I took the girl out for a walk in the residence complex, playing in its small park and the swimming pool. She seemed to be excited about this new place.

That evening, shortly after my husband returned from work, I had dinner ready and we three sat down at a small square table, ready to eat. The CD player was on, and this time was a tune called "Song of the Irish Whistle." We started eating as we listened to the music that reminded me of Chinese flute, a familiar slow and sweet flowing with gentle falls and rises. As the melodious sounds of flute went on, the girl, who had been quietly listening while eating her rice, suddenly put down her chopsticks. I asked her if she wanted more rice, she didn't respond; with her head bending over her bowl, she started sobbing, big drops of tears falling one by one into her bowl.

We were startled and asked her what was the matter. She then covered her face with both hands, bursting into a long and loud wail, as if she had been holding off something for quite a while and now finally let it out.

With the music still on, and between her sobbing, she cried: "I, I want to go home—I miss my home—I want to go home—"

My husband and I looked at each other, surprised and somewhat amused, trying to console her: baba and mama are here—this is also our home, isn't it?

Her head was still over her bowl, still sobbing, its sound becoming part of the "Song of the Irish Whistle."

That evening and every evening after that, we took her out to the big mall nearby where she played merry-go-round, enjoyed her special mint ice cream, picked her bears in Build-A-Bear Workshop, and made friends with other kids. For the rest of the summer there, she was her old happy self.

Yet, when the time came for us to return to Greensburg, no sooner had she hopped onto the backseat of our Trooper than she started another cry, this time a cry of joy: Hurray! Hurray! We are going home! We are going home!

With that word *home* and its cheerfulness, we headed back on Route 30, returning to those densely wooded hills, vast fields, roaming animals, and colorful farmhouses. For the entire ride, however, I couldn't help hearing, over and over again, the girl's crying for home in the midst of the "Song of the Irish Whistle."

For years that moment remains one of our family favorites, the moment when the sound of Irish flute accompanied a seven-year-old American girl of Chinese descent crying for her home in rural PA.

Now almost twenty years later, that little girl has left her rural home, first to college and then work, from Washington DC to New York City. But I know wherever she is, this home will always be part of her future ones; this land will continue to tell stories that become part of her life story.

The landscape, Lopez believes, is alive because of the stories. The stories from not only the landscape itself but also from all the creatures inhabiting that landscape.

With our only child leaving, our nest would soon be refilled by other children—the small creatures called red-belly-robins who, season after season, made their home and their life part of ours.

The first winter after our girl left home, we bought a new Christmas tree. With no intention of parting with the old one, which we got for her very first Christmas, I placed it in the inner corner of the front porch of the house we had recently moved into. The tree was only inches away from my front door. Summer after summer, the robins from different families had built on the top branches of the Christmas tree three six-inch-deep and four-inch-wide nests where they were homed, hatching, feeding their babies, and raising their families.

During those times, my front porch became a forbidden territory to the point where I couldn't even open the door. Each time I tried, which I do occasionally and out of absolute necessity, the parents would charge out of their nest, visibly upset, hovering over my front lawn just a few steps away, each telling me, in the loudest voice possible, with anxiety and urgency: please go away! Please go away! We need to feed our kids! They are waiting for us! Please leave us! Right now! Instinctively, I would talk back, OK! OK! Calm down! I am leaving! No worry! and retreat, gently closing the door, still peeking through the upper glass door, watching the parents flapping back to the nest, and listening to the noisily happy chirps of the little ones.

I would stand behind the door for a while longer, imagining how the parents and the kids enjoyed their family time in those sturdy and cozy nests and thinking of my own little bird who had flown away but now was brought back by these joyful red-belly birds.

It's a blessing—I learned a long time ago—to have birds live under one's roof.

Like my father's ancestorial house in his native village where I spent a few of my summers when young. The house, like many others, has as its ceiling the wooden beams where swallows built their nests. I remember seeing the swallows flying in and out of their nests, busy raising their families up there. At times, I even saw the little ones poo right on the floor or on the dinner table. My grandparents, like other villagers, would smile and say: no worry. Let them be. Good to have swallows at home. Good fortune. A blessing.

I believe that's what robins bring to our home—a blessing. Choosing to build their home as part of mine, they bless me with the songs of their joy and the stories of their lives.

Like the robins, other creatures—from small ones such as chipmunks, squirrels, rabbits to the bigger ones such as groundhogs, foxes, and deer—share their stories as they come and go across my front and backyard bordering on woods. In the daytime, the sound of squirrels, chipmunks, and rabbits playing from the crowning twig-tips with green cone, or inside the depth of the soil, or through the trees and bushes, ripples and sways like steady waves. In the nighttime, the sound of cicadas and crickets surge and ebb, like a small endless stream flowing in the dark or moonlit light.

To join the chorus of those feathered and furred creatures is the sound of a train whistle heard somewhere beyond those wooded hills. The railways are far away from where we live, but the sound feels much closer without any tall and high-rise buildings in between. The whistle, coming mostly from freight trains and one passenger train passing Greensburg to New York City, would transport me to a different time in my native home. Long before the era of those shining, soundless, bullet-like high-speed trains and passenger-only platforms, there were those steam-engine and green-cart trains slowly roaring into the railway stations flooded with people who were either arriving, or leaving, or welcoming, or sending off their loved ones. The whistle, long and loud, breaking through the thick white steam shooting straight from the locomotive, punctuates the sound of shouts, cries, good-byes, echoing in the air long before and after the train arrived and departed.

Sometimes, I would hear different kinds of whistles, like that of a car horn. It is no ordinary sound of car horn one would hear from impatient drivers in the city traffic. In fact, that sound might be heard only somewhere here in western PA where many towns had once been coal mining sites. That horn comes from an abandoned coal tunnel bridge. The tunnel, about fifty meters long and one car's width, is shaped like the letter S, which blocks the view of the cars at either end. Blowing a horn is the only way for either end to communicate: to remind the other end, I am coming, or I am here, please wait, be careful, I go first, or you go. The driver would keep the horn on in the tunnel as well as coming out to make sure to let the other end hear, or simply to say good-bye or a thank you.

This reassuring and resonating sound of horn breathes life into the abandoned tunnel, bringing back a lost time and the forgotten histories of the coal mines and the miners.

Not far from the coal tunnel flows Greensburg's only waterway, called Slate Creek that runs through the hills, fields, and resident areas. Though its origin and destination remain a mystery, the Creek, with its now rapid now gentle stream over which stand numerous small bridges, connects various communities in Greensburg, including my school, Pitt-Greensburg.

The Creek, running through the campus ever since its foundation in 1963, has become its own mother river. The legend goes that the Creek on the campus was once indeed like a river that could carry small boats. One year, because of weeks of nonstop rain, it swelled and flooded the entire school. Today, the part of the Creek on the campus is still about ten meters wide, with clear and rapid water meandering its way through the grasses and bushes, vegetation and wildflowers, and ancient-looking willow trees whose leaves swing over the surface of the water, dancing.

Over the Creek, there are three bridges. The longest one, about sixty meters long and three meters wide and built of wood with rails, stands right at the center of the campus, connecting the buildings, dorms, and classrooms on either side of the Creek. I don't need to cross the bridge to the other side of the campus for my classes, but I love to cross the bridge for the sake of crossing. Walking on the bridge, I can see in all directions—what is around, under, and beyond. I see my colleagues and students coming and going; I see the campus buildings on the hills and beside the woods; I see Creek water changing its color through different seasons—clear jade-like in the spring and summer, rainbow-like with red, yellow, green leaves in the autumn, and crystal white in the winter.

Each bridge-crossing gives me the joy of chanting those classic Chinese poems I learned by heart, the poems in which bridges whisper over the water, water sings to the willows, and willows chat with the passersby.

The sound of everything and everyone being part of everything and everyone else.

Which is one of many reasons why I am deeply drawn to the show *All Creatures: Great and Small* on PBS.

Not just the stunningly beautiful vast green fields and hills in Yorkshire Dales that always remind me those of Greensburg, but also, like James the veterinary surgeon says, it's people there and the love and kindness they show one another. James, who has come from the city of Glasgow where his parents expect him to return to, decides to settle down in Dale farmland and become part of that land and its people.

To "settle down," in my native language, Chinese, is to "take root." Having lived from one city to another all my life, I have indeed rooted in the rural town of Greensburg, still growing, learning to see the world through its lenses—that of rolling hills, dense forest, and open fields.

In old English and in German, the "burg" in Greensburg means a castle or fortress.

In Chinese, the word "rural" is an inseparable component of the phrase one uses to refer to one's native home.

So, Greensburg, the green castle, has become my native home.

This home speaks to me through its special rural sound and through its inhabitants—all creatures, great and small.

It is the sound that brings me what stories do for Lopez—a renewed sense of purpose in life, a rediscovered self, and a restored faith in the bond between the land and the human heart.

With these generous treasures my rural home graciously offers, I feel loved, strengthened, and always hopeful.

Work Cited

Lopez, Barry. "Landscape and Narrative." *Connections, Contexts, and Possibilities.* Ed. Stephen
Murabito. NJ, Prentice Hall, 2001.76-80.

MARJORIE MADDOX

Pennsylvania Round in Four Parts

I.

Before Pennsylvania, the world was flat, the distance between two horizons a straight view. In those other states, I walked a state-of-mind, linear but unlivable. Map coordinates located something less than inhale/exhale. Now place has something to do with oxygen horded in the limbs of hemlock and elm, with the way these mountains bulge with breath. Air blooms among such un-bashful blues and greens, darts with the dragonfly, drinks with the white-tailed deer. Always, it winds with the creeks, then glides over Allegheny curves to rise up with the hawks. When the firefly blinks, it is not an S.O.S. but a refrain from a mountain song so old you can hear the hills humming.

II.

The only light in the shotgun house is the steady blink of the TV. I've swept her job at the mill beneath the corners of a forty-year-old carpet, crammed his factory work in the closet they no longer open. But for years, I couldn't ignore the hum of what they didn't have, the absence they gave my husband in abundance. I can almost touch each wall with its peeling paper of orange watering cans as I hike between sheet-covered furniture lined up for the one clear view of a sit-com. Though I try to get comfortable, I can't. Even the air bunches up against itself between straight planes of plaster.

Outside the narrow windows, bricks block the coal-tinged breeze. Rusting lawn chairs clutter the neighbors' crumbling porches, from which out-of-work, middle-aged men stare at each other, and do nothing. Teens compete at squealing their make-shift hot rods down the thin strip of asphalt leftover between tightly parked pick-ups and hand-me-down four-doors. From the cracked sidewalk, barefoot girls in midriffs pause their hopscotch and wave.

I head instead to their backyard, where blooms border a six-by-four yard and spill over as geraniums and pansies, roses and Lazy Susans, tulips and marigolds. Humming birds nip nectar. Tomatoes bob from stalks tied-up with old panty hose. Lettuce proclaims victory over rabbits, and strawberries congratulate themselves for against-the-odds growth. My brown thumb, envious to the end, fingers joy.

III.

The doe and its fawn enter our backyard on the slant, kitty-corner themselves from rhododendron bush to magnolia. Theirs is a quiet joy, stepping just so from their hills into suburbia, the distance six hops of a skipped stone. They've forgotten to worry and remember this grass and the long limbs of our maple. They step easily between swing set and tool shed, detour around a half-finished game of croquet. Nurtured on grace, they politely turn their sleek necks to avoid our gaze. From behind glass, my children stare. They compare the soft sheen of the deers' fur to sketched likenesses in store-bought books. My husband warns them not to open the door, not to let the conditioned air out.

IV.

Beneath the tent flaps, my children and I breathe in the wild Pennsylvania air. The mountains, we say, are hugging the wind, the laurel so thick we could pick a thousand blooms. All evening we count the blinks of fireflies. We sense hawks circling the night clouds above our camp and bears obediently pausing between the zigzags of evergreens. We listen long into the dark until the drone of crickets leads us into dreams full of deer and ruffed grouse. Then we doze without worry, the curve of the world huddled about us as we breathe its crispness in.

In the chilled morning air, when we emerge from sleep and the tent door, it is—almost-surprisingly—just our backyard on the outside, our hammock waiting in the half-light of dawn. We think we hear the doe and her fawn, but it is my husband up on the patio, already flipping blueberry pancakes on the griddle. The country-style bacon sizzles with joy when we join him, humming our campfire rounds.

ABBY MINOR

Rooms

The bathroom must have been cold in winter—our house was heated by a woodstove, downstairs—but I remember it only in summer, the window open, a blue-green damp coming down off the Allegheny foothills. My mother's silver rings in a little box, her cotton balls and talcum powder, the two knobs for water, hot and cold, which came rushing into a cast iron tub. Among my mother's powers: she knew how much hot to run and how much cold. Standing beneath her in the shower, it was as when sunlight rips through grass and the soft blades move like a sea. When silver, green, and gold are braided on the surface of the deep. When I think of God I think of 1988: a woman on the cusp of forty showering in a scuffed-up tub; the view is from three-and-a-half feet.

***

On the day after my twenty-eighth birthday, I set up a room. It was the third bedroom in an old rented house; it was mostly empty; it was the middle of July, everywhere acid green. In the room were two windows mottled by leaf light; on the floor was a mattress with summer sheets. I brought in flowers, anise hyssop and chicory, sunflowers, bee balm, wild carrot, poppies. On a low table, on a lace cloth, I arranged speckled shells, a saggy doll handmade of bright silk, a photograph of my paternal great-grandmother at thirty, a card with a copy of a painting on the front: three artists, women working side by side in a desert of the southwest. The windows, the room itself, arranged and rearranged light, all kinds: splashed scraps, flickers on the walls and sheets, light shot through the curtains, spangling the floor.

I cut a man's white cotton t-shirt into strips and set these in a stack next to the mattress. I put my instructions in a purple folder and the folder beneath the stacked cotton. The brown paper bag, with the small orange prescription bottle inside, I also put next to the bed, on the floor.

And so I was writing: a story. A different story. A story about what Muriel Rukeyser calls "the relations that make us know the truth and the relations that make us know the beautiful." Also about what the great poet Frank Stanford says: "the law ain't nothing but bluebottle flies."

* * *

The law: not only the written codes, but silences and given forms. Laws that protect us not from violence, but from imagination and consciousness. For example:

Along U.S. Route 15 where it follows Pennsylvania's stretch of the Susquehanna River, a corridor of cinder-block strip clubs seems always to be open. You pass through this corridor to get to Harrisburg from Centre County, where I was born and still live. And to get to Route 15 from my house in the eastern part of the county, you travel south on two-lane roads through one valley after another. You pass hand-lettered signs attached to hay bales that warn, "Children Are a Blessing"; "Children Are a Gift from God." You pass, in the village of Mount Pleasant Mills, a low, windowless building on which is written in large, square black letters: FAMILY LIFE CENTER. Every time I drive this way, I try very hard to imagine the families, imagine the life. I try very hard to name the aura of the Family Life Center, which is identical to the aura of the strip club corridor. And I begin to feel the electricity of boundary, the tautening of law. The tautening of an annihilating choice: to be, as Adrienne Rich describes it, either "good or evil, fertile or barren, pure or impure." A law after which there is no self.

In a very small way, in a way that was certainly swallowed by history and the heat of July, I tried once to refuse to abide by that law and its precarious contradictions. I tried to live as a woman neither evil nor fecund. "It is to marginal and secret stories that we have to look," writes social historian Carolyn Steedman, "for any disturbance of the huge and bland assumption that the wish for a child largely structures femininity." And that is why, when my sweetheart and I drove to Harrisburg early on the day after my twenty-eighth birthday, I wore a slender, ankle-length cotton dress patterned with the silhouettes of cut-glass perfume bottles: my virtuous, my motherly, my feminine best.

I tried. Maybe I failed, or was failed. Like Stanford says. Nothing but bluebottle flies.

* * *

My nursery was also my mother's sewing room. The rug was nubby and dark red. The wallpaper had drawings of tiny kites with red, blue, and yellow sails. I remember clearly the view from the two windows, which looked south toward the long, soft line of the Bald Eagle Mountain ridge. I remember her sewing machine, its candle-like light, its engine-hum. Only much later would it occur to me that sewing, which as a child I thought of as all funk and freedom, is in the Judeo-Christian creation story the first act of civilization and, hence, the originary expression of shame. Cast out, the first woman and man make clothes. But back in that nubby-rugged nursery, hardly anything in my world had to do with shame—not nakedness, not sewing—and nearly everything had to do with those thick Appalachian summers, that zigzag house, that horsehair-and-plaster room.

On weekends, listening to her sew, I liked to crawl around in my mother's closet: a forest made of silk and wool, shadow and pattern, dresses and suits that moved vertically like trees. I'd pull the door to a crack, let in only a tall slice of light. I could crawl left or right for four or five feet in each direction; I could hear a wind, or maybe a rising creek.

I spent a lot of time in that closet; what did I do? Made things up, laid in a heap of shoes. Messed with my mother's green suitcase, a large suitcase lined with sheer, cream-colored material. It had a spin lock, and interior straps for securing folded clothes. It was that suitcase from which my wicked alter-ego, Tanya from New Orleans, emerged as from a portal. (My parents had lived in New Orleans for many years; there was a picture of them in the French Quarter tall and lean, dressed in dark clothes). As the story went, when Tanya came and did mischief, I slept locked in the suitcase, curled like an innocent. But the suitcase only worked one way; I never woke up in New Orleans. I still don't know why I equated being locked up with running away.

* * *

In those days after my twenty-eighth birthday, in that room filled with scattered sun, I wrote:

I was a violet bone
singular
in accord
with the lit world, July:
it was like giving birth
to an open field
an entire absence shaped
like an acre of light.

I didn't have much to do; I was hiding. After I placed the four unassuming tablets gently inside myself, after I lay there alone with flowers and seashells, waiting; after I closed my eyes, and my sweetheart held me—after the heaviest blood came, I didn't have much to do. I washed my cotton strips, I watched the light grow and change, I watched the flowers flare and scatter pollen down on the lace cloth. Still bleeding some and tired, I imagined all those scraps of light as pieces I could pick up off the floor, stitch a flickering quilt or dress. And I remembered how in middle school I was once or twice called "ugly girl" by milk-faced boys. How, like all girls without "normal" hair, I had wished then for normal hair. How I had harbored a melancholy fear of being found unattractive to men, a terror of invisibility.

Now, stowed away in the hot crease of July, I thought about being invisible, and to whom, and about what exactly it was I had been so scared of back then, in that long, linoleum-tiled public school hall where the word "ugly" had hovered, where some small part of me had agreed to go in fear of it always. Had agreed to bow in grief before it always. When the people in Harrisburg stood with their signs and screamed, when they stood and prayed, when they stood and shouted out, that part of me split the wires and—exhausted, starving—finally slipped away.

* * *

In a progressive book on women's health, I read that one way to avoid "post-abortion trauma" is to have sex only with men whose children you'd be willing to bear. The idea is offered as a counterweight to "casual" lovemaking, a kind of retro-radical focus on the sacred link between sex and fertility. The efficacy of this approach for women who may not want to bear children, the magnificence or shortcomings of their male sexual partners aside, is not discussed. I can only conclude that such women do not exist. I can only conclude that if one truly comprehends the sacred nature of sex and fertility, one will, under the right circumstances, wish to bear a child (or, at least, be "willing" to). I can only conclude that I do not exist.

In many obvious ways, I do not exist. I do not exist in the silence at the other end of the line when I call my doctor's office to ask about medical abortion; I do not exist when the receptionist finally suggests that I get a prescription for Plan B. I do not exist when, a few days later, the soft-spoken, unnamed doctor calls from Harrisburg to counsel me; as he is legally required to do, he offers a pamphlet on fetal development and explains that my options include adoption and parenting. I do not exist in the ensuing post-counsel waiting period predicated on my instability. I do not exist in the rural borough of eight hundred where I live and wait, where starred-and-striped flags crack in the heat and the church bells play at noon "Were You There When They Crucified my Lord?," where my sweetheart and I look up bullet-proof vests and wake weeping in the night. I do not exist in the nearby university town, where you can't get an abortion, but where you can choose from among the most advanced fertility treatment programs, two palatial OB-GYN groups, and three religious, anti-abortion "pregnancy counseling" centers. The counseling centers fly American flags and inhabit sturdy old bungalows, in a downtown neighborhood with streetlamps out front.

But I also disappear in less obvious ways. I catch myself blurring into shadow; some mountain just beyond view casts its long, peculiar shadow. What mountain? What shadow? "That's a hard choice," more-or-less sympathetic people say, and I disappear. A friend who works in women's health says, "That's a hard choice." "That's a hard choice," says someone else, and "was it hard to decide?" says another, and "that's really hard." And what do you do when someone is putting an ill-fitting dress on you, and you are grateful to be clothed at all but a shadow is falling and you are a landed fish, wearing a dress, drowning in air?

Considering the windowless clinic; considering the week of waiting and the two-hour drive; considering another woman's tires slashed and the AAA guy saying, "Yeah, we come here all the time"; considering the Apostle Paul's promise that "woman will be saved through bearing children"; considering the story in which God is not an adult woman but an embryonic male; can I really agree that abortion itself is "hard"?

A hard choice it was not, but the bluebottle flies nearly ate me alive.

* * *

For as long as I can remember I've been drawing—first with crayons and then with colored pencils and then with watercolor paint and ink—more or less the same thing. I draw women; I draw women alone. Women in dresses, women standing next to trees or towering blossoms or little houses half their height. Solitary women, women who live in fields of red or magenta, ringed with washes of lavender and cool green. I've made hundreds of these drawings, maybe a thousand over the years. In one I made over two decades ago, I drew my mother coming from the bath, her arms and breasts akimbo, her head hair and crotch hair twin tangles of black fire. I look at these drawings now and think of each one as a room, imaginary spaces in which a woman's solitude is neither selfish nor crazy nor lethal, but holy.

"I want to have kids," says a friend, "because I want to be part of making more joy in the world." The shadow falls, it casts a peculiar tinge over my drawings, and it strikes me that we speak of childbearing not as subjective and mutable but as synonymous with generosity and joy; that childbearing's unexamined monopoly on joy compresses the scope of possibility, becomes a violence. Someone asks, "Why do the women in your drawings always look sad?" They never looked sad to me.

It may be true, as the hay bales say, that children are a gift from God, but my own desire not to bear a child, like any fully-fledged desire, was a garden—incarnate, rooted, indisputable and beautiful in its complexity. And the grief I felt—still sometimes feel—had less to do with loss than with being cast beyond the boundaries of what's heard. I think of that room I set up in July; I wonder, locked up or running away? Writes the poet Susan Howe, "Rungs between escape and enclosure are confusing and compelling." I don't have a magic suitcase anymore, and I'm not sure where it would take me if I did. Where am I and where would I try to go? Cast out, casting in, here among bee balm and poppies, ringed with washes of cool green. I'm making clothes with pieces of light.

BATHSHEBA MONK

A Rock and a Hard Place

The past and its geographic setting, the motherlode for an artist, at some point in the artist's career becomes worn with retelling, hyperbole, then inevitably is grown over with irrelevancy. The threads that connect those origin stories eventually dry rot.

My own stories of Pennsylvania coal dust and steel forges—at first exotic, then fascinating, then finally repugnant in equal measure to the official literary world roosting in Brooklyn—soon unraveled from their physical setting which had rusted out of literal existence. The ideas which came out of that formation became not only barely comprehensible to those who never experienced black collar survival, but "problematic" as a student informed me, dismissing my work.

I was out of time. Out of context.

As an analog, unaddicted, straight female writer of European cultural birthright, it has been a tough ten years trying to reclaim my audience, no matter how rich my story pool and no matter how hard I labor to plow a row in my native soil. My audience has migrated to the Polish Cooking page on Facebook where among the dueling recipes for sauerkraut soup and pierogies, a rogue poster—me!—tries to slip in pictures of grandparents holding jars of pickles, dill and cucumber, both nurtured between rows of coal ash in a coal patch outside of Hazelton, Pennsylvania, before the moderator gets hip to this breach in protocol—no personal history!—and throws me off the forum.

The thing about writers is that we can't shut up. If the Pennsylvania of my youth had revoked my literary membership, I would find the servants' entrance.

I spent New Year's Eve with my husband, the writer Paul Heller, and friends in the Delaware Water Gap. We wanted to hear jazz at the Deer

Head Inn, a place I'd heard about but never had visited because at an hour and a half away from Allentown, my current home, a return trip at one in the morning after a couple of glasses of wine seemed too daunting. The state troopers in Monroe County are notorious for diligence after the bars close.

We booked rooms on the steep fourth floor of an 1850 building sans elevator, and we arrived early, hoping to see some of the physical beauty of the area before dark, but it was too foggy. As we were way early for dinner and New Year's Eve entertainment, we schlepped our bags up the crooked stairs and decided to get a cup of coffee and a piece of pie at the Mt. Bethel Diner, a couple of miles away.

Our friends, David and Karle Schwartz, brought along a book, *Annals of the Former World* by John McPhee. There were twenty pages that detailed the geologic history of the Delaware Water Gap that they wanted us to read. David had read several pages to us when we stopped for lunch on the way up and now, unbelievably, we were hooked on its fascinating plot about limestone resistance forming the Kittatinny Ridge during the Silurian Age, which we were now improbably *sitting on*, enjoying warmed-up apple pie, bottomless cups of coffee, and fabulous waitress banter as we alternated reading it aloud.

The Silurian Age was roughly 420 million years ago.

We couldn't drive the straight-line down Route 611 from Mt. Bethel to the Delaware Water Gap as there had recently been a rockslide and the road was closed. Indefinitely we were told. They had found other structural problems when they removed the rocks. Shrugs when we asked when it would open again.

We tried to get a look at the ridge when we drove back to the inn, but it was still foggy, visibility a literal stone's throw. The only lights were the speeding red and white lights on Interstate 80 which slashes through and defines the Gap.

The now dark town of Delaware Water Gap itself seemed deserted, half-hearted Christmas lights blinking through the fog, vacancy signs in the nearby motel. No other living creatures. The dining room of our inn, empty tables decorated with New Year's hats and noisemakers, the deserted bandstand with Yamaha baby grand and drum kit, all acoustic, anachronistic. I felt at home. I'm a dinosaur, too.

We joked that it was the perfect set-up for a murder mystery.

My novelist brain immediately traveled to the nooks and crannies of our environs, wondering how many bodies lay unclaimed. I have recently rethought my bourgeois idea that law enforcement pursues all missing persons and murder allegations. Maybe if your name was famous on Instagram the authorities might be compelled to closure. Otherwise not.

A few years ago, I took a trip with my brother to find our roots in the coal region. None of our family names were on ship manifests or in any of the logs at ports of entry, even accounting for the practice of anglicizing Eastern European names, which authorities found foreign and unpronounceable with their spare use of vowels. Lucky for us, we are tall fair-haired people, which allowed us to pass, especially when we married out of our ungainly surnames.

We found the graves of the Hzbinkos, Herbinko by the time my maternal grandmother married in West Hazelton, only sixty miles west of the Delaware Water Gap on Route 80 on the western edge of the Poconos. But it might have been a different planet. Still, they had claimed their earth. Complete with ostentatious monument and little cement lambs where the babies were laid.

We found the deed to the old Victorian mansion in Junedale which my grandparents had somehow bought. They were coal miners and I always wondered how people who ate government cheese and peanut butter and received 64 cents a month miners' pension could afford that house as well as the next-door house which my grandmother rented to boarders; especially considering that my grandfather had been in a mine cave-in right before my mother was born and so their miners' income was lost. He survived, but couldn't work after the accident., and disability insurance was a few decades in the future. My grandparents' plight was a normal part of life in the coal region.

The deed told all. My grandmother's sister, a family beauty, had married a Scottish landowner who owned most of Junedale and sold both the mansion and the adjoining house to my grandmother for a dollar.

My brother and I found the house in West Hazelton where another sister, another Hzbinko, lived with her then-unmarried brothers and where she reportedly accidentally fell to an early death from the third-floor window. My brother and I stared at that window, an attic window, narrow and high, and we said, at the same time, "She was pushed."

There were unclaimed bodies here, all right. Here, there, and everywhere. Becoming part of the geological history. Waiting to tell their stories. Waiting to be woven into the narrative.

Self-aware homo sapiens have only populated the Delaware Water Gap for 10,000 years. The Lenape were the first to have even an oral history. They knew that the river, the Delaware, which was more than 10,000 years ago was flowing in the opposite direction, had forced itself through the unstable rock formations, forming the Gap. They told stories about it. Modern geologists using their picks and hammers confirmed the rumors.

The Lenape had welcomed the Dutch as oddly dressed fellow humans who had come to mine the copper that someone had erroneously claimed was there in the early 1600s. The Dutch also trapped, hunted, felled forests, and took it as their right to claim the entire area as theirs. When the Lenape realized that they were being snookered, they began a pogrom, coming out of a hidden tunnel in the Kittatinny ridge, massacring settlers, then retreating back into the tunnel. It took years for the Dutch to find that tunnel.

When they did it was over, of course. For the Lenape.

During the Silurian Age and the thousand million years before that, the earth was busy moving and grooving to rockslides and dramatically fluctuating temperatures, stratifying layers of both incompatible and accepting materials that would form the staging area for humans. Geologists talk of these slides happening every million years, making the rockslide that closed Route 611 a once-in-a-million-year event.

The entertainment on New Year's Eve at the Deer Head was a trio led by jazz singer, Giacomo Gates. Giacomo had worked as a construction worker out of high school in Connecticut, operating earth-moving equipment before heading north to work on the Alaskan Pipeline for twelve years, building the structure for oil to be transported from the geological swamp that creates petroleum to the lower 48. He was discovered singing in the Fairbanks Jazz Festival by Sarah Vaughn.

The jazz pianist, Tomoko Ohno, was born in Japan. An international talent, she transforms a native American music form to a giddily transplendent level.

Paul Rostock, the bass player, plays with every notable jazz musician on the East Coast.

None of the trio had played together before that night. It was exciting to hear what they created together. The joy of listening to people who speak different musical dialects of the same language.

Us too. We met people from all over, our common denominator a love of jazz and a good time, and the wherewithal to find it. Nobody we talked to, including us, was native to this patch. But it felt like home.

The Victorian mansion that my grandparents bought for a dollar was razed by one of my sixty-four cousins who still live in the area. I think he inherited it, but nobody in our family questioned his possession of it. He and his partner, who married in a vintage military-themed wedding as soon as gay marriage was legal in Pennsylvania, built a one-story house on the yard where my grandparents grew dill and cucumbers.

I wouldn't recognize him if we bumped shoulders in the street.

On New Year's Day, the inn served us brunch and we met some New Yorkers who were going to retire here. David and Paul had roots in New York City and there's nothing like homies for a joyful reunion which we planned to repeat when the Delaware Water Gap had a jazz festival in the fall.

We drove as far as we could down Route 611 to Kittatinny where the first tourist hotel in the area was erected in the nineteenth century. The painter George Innes had stayed there and his work made the area famous. The Kittatinny hotel housed at the end of its tenure 250 rooms of people.

Karle found a covered over path across the road that led up worn stone stairs paralleling a waterfall that originated in an underground stream; part of the relentless, thousands of millions year old underground movement that caused earlier geological shifts and the recent rockslide.

There was a Pennsylvania State Park information poster telling us that this is indeed where the Kittatinny hotel once stood. There is no evidence that a hotel ever existed. We could more easily picture Lenape than stiff-necked Dutchmen and tulle-skirted tourists.

The sun has burned off the fog and we could see the Gap from the overlook. It is geologically and visually stunning, the relentless traffic on Route 80 at this geologic moment notwithstanding.

We got in our car for the ride home, Karle talking of eventually retiring here. Connections already threading their way into our hundred-million-year mental narrative.

MATT PERAKOVICH

The Bear

Twenty months after the accident, I am watching a black bear run in slow motion. I've just downshifted up three miles of Red Rock Mountain, and on this flat stretch of rural highway in late September, the shadows of the telephone poles are longer than the poles are high. Though I perceive the bear in slow motion, I know the animal must be loping along at a decent clip, kinetic chain somehow both clunky and fluid. Right away, I am sure that our vectors will intersect: the bear's rush toward ten thousand acres of mountain forest on the other side, oblivious to the road that moats it off, and me in my car on that very road, singing along to Arcade Fire and traveling at a reluctant pace, well below the speed limit, to a graveyard shift at the Job Corps Center. Collision feels inevitable. I hit the brakes hard and steady, but I am resolved not to swerve wildly. When my front bumper strikes the adult black bear, which must be 250, 300 pounds, the impact is softer than I expect. The bear, pushed forward, splays in the air, almost floating, limbs out, before tumbling, rolling twice until, in the brush past the berm, it finds itself back on all fours and, like a running back shaking off a hit, gallops off again in the direction it was moving before I ever came along. Now the road is empty except for me, so I slow the car down, and the engine sounds alright. In less than a mile, I will be at work and then I'll look for damage. I rev, the car responds, so I keep going too.

* * *

Let's just get this out of the way: sixteen years ago, on a Friday night in January, I was driving my wife and our three kids from our home outside of a tiny town called Rohrsburg to her mother's about an hour north when I hit black ice on an S-curve, skidded across the other lane, and hit an embankment. I wasn't driving fast and the car wasn't damaged, but before I could right the vehicle, an on-coming full-sized pick-up smashed into the rear passenger side: the sound of breaking glass, the car whipped abruptly ninety degrees, then stillness.

From all I could tell, I was still fine; I opened my door and stepped into a noiseless din of activity. I reached in and unbuckled my five-year-old son, who was sitting behind me. "Are you okay?" I asked and he nodded, though I could see he was scared. I then helped my eight-year-old daughter, who had been sitting in the backseat's middle and was now up and walking, though she complained that her back hurt. My wife, who wasn't wearing her seat belt, was already out of the car, walking around, hugging the kids, looking them over. Finnias, who had turned two last month, was still in his car seat and his face was covered in blood. I figured he had broken his nose and had perhaps lost some teeth. I lifted him from his seat and handed him to his mother and then other cars came on the scene and ambulances were called and then someone saw Finn and radioed Geisinger Medical Center to send a Life Flight helicopter. Who knows how long it was but soon the helicopter was there and gone, then an ambulance arrived and took my wife and my older son and daughter, and I stayed with the car, which looked like it had been punched by the steel fist of a mad god. I waited for the tow truck and I talked to the state trooper but I kept wondering what happened.

The man who towed my car to the body shop kindly dropped me off at my house, where I dialed my mother, my father, and my mother-in-law to tell them what happened and not to worry, that I was optimistic that everyone would be okay. I then called the hospital and spoke to a man with a practiced consoling voice who told me the kids were all getting cat scans as we spoke. I took our second car and drove slowly, fists clenching the steering wheel, talking to myself all the way to Bloomsburg down 487 and then over on Route 11 to Geisinger, convincing myself all over again that everything was going to be fine. When I pulled up to the emergency entrance, my wife was waiting for me on the other side of the glass door. Her face was twisted up. Her mouth moved with words.

* * *

Twenty-four hours before the crash, with her new digital camera, my wife had recorded Finn eating ziti. The clip is twenty-one seconds long: he has two pieces of ziti on his fork, removes one with his left hand and puts it in his mouth, chews and swallows, then licks his marinara-stained fingers with an audible smack of delight. Then he grabs the other piece of pasta off the fork, stuffs it in his mouth and begins to chew, but then sees that his mother is recording him and so he chews more dramatically, delightfully. At the end of the clip, he turns his eyes towards me off camera and smiles, as if to report, "Am I not the most beautiful thing you have ever seen?" For months afterward, I watch this clip at least once a day.

* * *

One dream soon after is set in the Benton Fire Hall. Though no banner hangs to indicate this, I know that I am at a party celebrating local teenage time travelers. Finn is chasing his brother and sister around the room, up and down the three aisles of cafeteria tables left from bingo earlier that day. White streamers hang from the drop ceiling, and a long table holds a banquet of pretzels and chips, meatballs and rolls, bright red punch. Silver stars framed photographs of local middle school do-gooders. When I notice one of them right in front of me, a twelve-year-old kid with short brown hair, I reach out and shake his hand. His hand feels like putty, then pebbles, then ash, and he announces, "I have to go." He dematerializes mid-handshake and he's gone, whatever smoke or dust that promised to remain sucked into some rip in the cosmos that closed with the sound of a kiss. No one makes a big deal about it, including me, and that's when it dawned on me—the me watching the me in the dream: Finn had been transported from before the accident to the now after. His death hung in the past like cancer does for a survivor. The twelve-year-old boy was the one, the noble nobody who goes back into the burning building to save the baby, only the burning building is now a moment in time.

Now in the dream, we are five minutes before the accident, when I filled the tank of my Subaru at a gas station in Benton. I am making faces to Finnias in his car seat and he is making them back at me through his long blond hair that fell into his face, when the kid from the fire hall appears right behind me and taps my shoulder.

"I need your son," he tells me, so matter of fact that I don't even start laughing. But of course, I hesitate. Who gives their son over to anyone, let alone some strange twelve-year-old kid. "I can't tell you why, but you must believe me. He needs to come with me," he tells me, in a voice so sure I consider it.

And because I know what happens next, I wake up. And because when I wake, I am in what happens next, I try to fall back asleep, to chase the dream down again.

* * *

For years after the accident, I believed the loss of my son was visible in my every movement and gesture, that it was obvious that I might start sobbing at any time, at the grocery store, in conversation, walking down the street. I felt achingly fragile around everyone, strangers even. Maybe strangers especially. Who knows, maybe they'd know what it felt like too.

These are not easy things to write, but the telling doesn't feel impossible either. It's a victory that feels cold, but it is also a reminder that time's bottomless appetite will consume even infinite sadness.

* * *

I have spent most of my career, if you can call it that, as an adjunct writing instructor. Some semesters, work dried up, and that meant I needed to find something else. Staring down one of those semesters about a year after the accident, I decided to look for another job. Because it was full-time, close by and promised health care, I applied for a position as a residential advisor at the Red Rock Job Corps.

I already knew about the Job Corps, having grown up not far from Red Rock. The Job Corps' sixty-acre campus is tucked into a corner of Ricketts Glen, the thirteen thousand-acre state park famous for its Falls Trail, where you can see twenty-one waterfalls over the course of a four-mile loop. Part of Lyndon Johnson's War on Poverty, the Job Corps program was intended to help low-income students earn their GED and learn a trade. There are over 120 Job Corps locations across the country and I bet Red Rock is one of the most isolated.

A high school friend's father ran the art program at Red Rock, but for the most part, the place was a mystery to most kids in our rural community. For one thing, the Job Corps students rarely strayed from campus and when they left, to go shopping, say, or to see a movie, these mostly urban kids were allowed to venture only as far as the relatively small city of Wilkes-Barre or the decidedly small town of Bloomsburg. Sullivan County, where I grew up, had one traffic light and no town with a population of over 900 people, and was 98 percent white. The Red Rock kids were different. They came from Philly, Allentown, Harrisburg, and recruiters sold Job Corps as a pseudo-college setting, where they might buckle down and focus for a year or eighteen months and then go home with a future. They rarely interacted with the surrounding community, supposedly so they could keep focused but also, no doubt, because of racism. If, on some rare occasion, the students at the Job Corps were discussed by locals, they used dog whistle undertones, called them "city kids" and some people, more overtly, would complain that we didn't need "that element" around here.

The director who interviewed me seemed impressed that a "college professor" wanted to serve as residential advisor at the Job Corps. I came to the interview with some idea that I could offer intellectual guidance, a strong belief in the power of education, that I would pass along secrets to upward mobility. After all, I had gone from a working-class family to teach in college classrooms (as an adjunct, but still). I got the job.

The only problem: the commute forced me to drive past the spot of the accident every day, to and from work. And every day, a little pain shot through me, some mix of sadness, a tinge of sublime terror, and a heaping dose of guilt. I think now that I was doing it on purpose, building a callus or some nonsense like that.

After school hours at the Job Corps, the students were plenty bored living in the middle of nowhere. Every week a couple fights would break out, but mostly it was quiet. The students played video games in their rooms or watched TV in the lounge. A few of the students had kids of their own and shared with me grainy photos of infants on their flip phones. Most of the time, I felt like a glorified hall monitor. I did half-hearted room inspections once a week, I enforced lights out at ten. In the morning, in the obnoxious manner of an upbeat father, I woke up those students sleeping past their alarm. Wakey, wakey, eggs and bakey.

After working the third shift, I had time to make it home so I could take my kids to school. And because I was in the habit of winding down after work with a drink, and because night shift, when I got back to the house, I poured myself a glass or two of whiskey at nine in the morning to help bring sleep, so I could do it all over again the next night.

I don't remember much about my work duties the night I hit the bear, but I do remember the shift seemed to stretch on forever. After lights out, when the hours were the longest, I couldn't stop thinking about the bear, both the physics problem of the accident, and how that affected the probability and severity of the animal's suffering. Could a bear survive with a hip fracture? What about internal bleeding? The fact that it kept running was surely a good sign, right? At 2 A.M., I walked outside to smoke and to stare into the darkness beyond the orange halogen lights. Were it not for the generator whirring, would I hear the animal's moans deep in the forest? But, really, what could I do? I was a destroyer.

In his landmark essay, "Why Look at Animals?", John Berger writes, "The animal has secrets which, unlike the secrets of caves, mountains, seas, are specifically addressed to man." Exploring the existential difference between man and animal, he identifies that "narrow abyss of non-comprehension," and argues that we have sacrificed a piece of ourselves by moving animals further from the center of human experience. Are these secrets still passed to us, those of consciousness and instinct, light and shadow? Are we alive in our surroundings, or apart from them, isolated in a world of our own construction?

Fractured and bleeding, the bear kept running. Did I know that I was broken? Did I care? How much control did I have, how much agency? So much of my life, then, felt knee-jerk, instinctual. I was at velocity, barreling toward my own void, which felt like certainty, like calm. Less than two months later, I would go to the clinic with what I thought was the swine flu. The doctor said I had a resting heart rate of 140 beats per minute and diagnosed me with congestive heart failure. I spent three days in the hospital. Soon after, I blew up my marriage.

* * *

Grief is a spell made from beyond language. How it is woven into us fascinates me, obsesses me, the way it mutates and darkens our lives, and how sometimes, ideally, we soften around loss. What does it open up inside of us? What does it invite in?

Finnias would have turned eighteen this month. Imagining him as a young man is not impossible; he looked a lot like his older brother when he was an infant, and I imagine so much of the same genetic material would have carried forward. His brother is nearly six foot now and serious, but still, his long hair gets in his eyes.

However, in the few dreams I have had of him in the last decade, Finn has remained two years old. Usually, we are just hanging out in some broken off piece of time that could have been yesterday or some Sunday from his past. We play. I hold him on my lap and read to him. The dreams no longer bear the portent of the dreams right after the accident when I used to wake up and cry. Now, when I wake, I am just grateful for the mysterious frequencies of my unconscious, for its misfires and nonsense songs, how it holds it all together, how on that dark highway, we intersect.

PJ PICCIRILLO

On Leaving

I've always been indignant about living under a microscope. Those of us from the Pennsylvania "T," that Alabama between Pittsburgh and Philadelphia, as James Carville so disparagingly stereotyped both us and the people of Appalachia's southern border in 1986, are too often specimens. We're studied then treated in various ways for the disease of isolation. We need saved from ourselves.

Carville and others behind the microscope typically ascribe us a coarse and myopic field of view, suggesting we're backward, racist, and ignorant. Some of that can be traced to the assumptions and generalizations made about the people of Appalachia after media and—I can think of no better term—do-gooders flooded this part of the world in response to the writings of Harry Caudill in the 1960s and 70s.

The term "Pennsyltucky," like Carville's Alabama comparison, had emerged by that time. It speaks to the several pigeonholes, based on a matrix of geography, livelihood, folkways, and population density, into which the studiers behind the microscope place regions within Appalachia.

I do not despise this word Pennsyltucky; sans the pigeonholing, it celebrates an ethos of self-sufficiency that many Western Pennsylvanians carried to Kentucky after the Whiskey Rebellion of the 1790s. What I do despise is how it has been appropriated as an ivory tower of sophistication from which people behind the microscope can inspect us with a mixture of pity and disgust.

By my observation, most of us in this neck of the woods prefer to be left alone. And by our own metric, we fair pretty well. We do this, I am proud to say, with a disproportionate allotment of money from Harrisburg. Or so our legislators tell me.

But by many standards, for us to be healthy, wealthy, and wise, we need to either become like the other two parts of the state or leave for places like the other two parts of the state. Interestingly, over the past several years, during an inconvenient pandemic which deprived people outside the T of urbane activities, I have seen a phenomenal increase in them flocking to our small towns, parks, and points of interest to vacation, recreate, buy "cabins," and even live.

Nevertheless, Pennsylvanians from the T, particularly writers and other artists after having gained commercial success, have followed the standards and left. From America's largest metropolis, they've looked back with an ostensibly sympathetic but clearly disapproving eye. Sometimes their work is a commentary on their former neighbors that is downright condescending. We're typecast at best as quaint, the threshold beyond which is sophistication. No round characters to be had here. Still, they've sold a lot of books and art centered on, or at least looking at, this place they've left. This smells of snake oil.

It's hard for me to adequately convey my revulsion for this phenomenon without it sounding like sour grapes. Instead, I will tell you the story of an artist who did leave—though there's a twist—a person who possessed such a beautiful soul that the world tried all it could to destroy her. The ironies of her life will speak to my point.

Eunice Mildred (LonCoske) McCloskey was born in Ridgway, in Elk County, in 1904. She was an exceptional child from a large but modest family, her father a borough worker and her mother a seamstress. Eunice possessed a vivid imagination, all her senses attuned to the natural wonder and beauty of her Clarion River valley, here at the edge of what would become the Allegheny National Forest in 1923. As a child, Eunice developed a sharp ear and eye for the composite character of her community of immigrants, industrial barons, and derelicts; she relished Ridgway's diversity of folkways and traditions, its Americana architecture and its slums, and even as a little girl, she became as fascinated and charmed by its sinners as by its saints, by its poor as by the sons and daughters of founders who lived in intricately trimmed Victorian mansions constructed of the rich Allegheny timber milled at Ridgway's world famous Hyde Murphy Company. In short, her keen heart fell in love with the place she came from, and in a way that would prove not to be so naïve as the studiers might think.

She wrote later in life that it was by the sky—a subject that would fascinate her—that she understood how there are no limits to the imagination, as there are no walls in eternity.

Eunice could not wait to learn to read, and once she did, her mind became a passageway for literature and art and history. As a student, she carried a notebook and sketchpad everywhere, and against many odds, upon her high school graduation, entered Columbia to major in poetry and English.

In New York, Eunice spent her free time with the artists and Bohemians of Washington Square. In the spring of her freshman year, she visited home. She surprised her family with a fiancé, the son of a wealthy Persian merchant she'd met in Greenwich Village. She was destined for refinement and wealth.

During that visit, something profound happened to Eunice McCloskey. Something I think may have happened to many people from places like Ridgway, Pennsylvania. She saw her place suddenly from the perspective of a changed person, or so she thought she was. Everything about her town was smaller, a luster had faded. She remarked in her autobiography, *So Dear to My Heart*, "Such small and dingy stores." Having been away for a year, she said, "I saw it without my rosy spectacles; it had peace and a quaint charm, but it had provincialism, which is demanding. It hems one in, in religion and manners and clothes. Conversation among women was mostly gossip. They pretended they were big frogs in a big puddle. I guess they had to do this to survive a hundred miles from nowhere, with nobody to impress but one another."

But that new perspective was not so simple for someone as discerning as Eunice McCloskey. She understood irony. By this change, Eunice for the first time questioned what she had taken for granted: that her place was big and shiny. And so she grew suspicious of the filter she had gained in Manhattan, and she wondered if the world, too, saw her place through this suspect filter. I think she was indignant.

Eunice McCloskey was one tough woman. I admire her immensely. She stood up for the independence of thought and the inherent power of any human—man or woman.

Eunice would not only forsake Columbia after that visit—not to mention a cultural scene where she'd already rubbed elbows with famous poets and painters—she broke off her engagement with the extremely handsome and debonair man who would have ensured her a life of comfort.

She had already been a star student, had published poetry in national magazines. But something was calling Eunice, and she returned to Ridgway and married an appliance repairman. They bought a fixer-upper house, and while she painted and wrote, they lived a hardscrabble life.

She asked once ". . . is it that humans bear the print of some spot on this revolving globe upon their hearts, never to lose it?"

Over the next 50 years, Eunice McCloskey created more than four thousand oils, watercolors, acrylics, pen and ink drawings, and etchings on her dining room table. She wrote seventeen books of nonfiction, novels, and poetry. Her short fiction appeared in the *Ladies Home Journal* and *McCall's.* She was awarded three national poetry and arts prizes. She was a member of the International Institute of Arts and Letters, National League of American Pen Women, the Pennsylvania Federation for Women, the Philadelphia Art Alliance, and directed the Associated Artists of Pittsburgh. The list goes on. Eight hundred of her paintings have hung in sixteen states, in Europe, the national museum, and the Carnegie Museum of Art. Eunice McCloskey was honored at three Whitehouse tea receptions. Carl Sandberg went out of his way to visit her in Ridgway. She became known, for a while, as the "Grandma Moses of Pennsylvania."

Eunice never took an art lesson, and she accomplished her work after having suffered deafness and without full use of her dominant hand—a train had hit a car she rode in at the age of twenty.

The result was a style that appears at first childlike. But that was her brilliance in full display. The primitiveness of technique, the quaintness of her subjects—company picnics; family reunions; her mother's childhood; a courthouse; and time and again, her beloved Ridgway—was an intentional naiveté that set her apart from the idiom of her contemporaries. She felt a great need to remind us of our nearest blessings and neighbors. She was a champion of poor people, natural places, trees in particular, and women—but in action, not simple activism.

Make no mistake, Eunice recognized the closed-mindedness of parochialism. But she never condescended because she was one of her people by choice. She did not leave her home to pontificate about it from afar. She lived out something that a very smart person told me: *You can't change things from the outside.* Always the actor, not the activist, she admitted she, too, was a sinner and could write only from the place of the sins she understood.

Eunice died in 1983 in her self-proclaimed "Lilly of the Valley." But that's not the end of this story.

I recently found a haunting clipping of an interview from a year before Eunice died. She said, "Some of the townspeople like me, but some think of me as a crackpot." Still, she said that though she had tried, she had long ago come to realize that she could not create anywhere but "in this isolated valley." She said that one day, the Village Improvement Association of Ridgway would secure a building and house her books and many of her paintings, which she had earmarked for "the children of Ridgway." Everything Eunice had created had been for her people so she could help them appreciate the beauty and importance of their place and themselves.

That Village Association is long gone, and thirty-eight years later, I, a fan of her work, helped Eunice's niece sort through paintings, clippings, books, manuscripts, and photographs, which had been stored in a rented basement room in anticipation of a museum that would never be. Her niece told me that no historical society or museum had any interest in most of the items, and so she distributed them to anyone she could find who would take them.

Eunice is just about forgotten in American art, unknown through Pennsylvania, hardly a memory in Ridgway. But who's to blame but us as we evaluate ourselves through the eyes of outsiders?

There must be a message in Eunice's decision. In teaching creative writing—if such can be taught—I offer that the resolution is often already there if the story is crafted well enough. You just need to search for it.

So I arrive at this: The recurring theme in Eunice McCloskey's life and art is humility. Already on the level of its subjects, her work simply revealed her people, warts and all, with complete, unabashed and, at times, cruel honesty. It was detached from any personal or social pretensions, indifferent to others' yardsticks.

If I've learned anything from the examples of the masters, art can attain something close to truth only if you take yourself out of it, if you trust it to speak for itself. Eunice's gift to her audience was not motivated by sentimentalism, agendas, trends, or sanctimony. Certainly not money. Her renderings neither censured nor patronized. And she never attempted to transcend her place. For Eunice understood that to be true to her subject, and to herself, she had to remain where she would smell like the other sheep.

You may argue that Eunice simply didn't have it. Or that had she stayed in New York and written with sympathy and superiority about the people she'd left, she would at least have sold more books and paintings. She'd be remembered today.

This is where her life story speaks for itself. Eunice knew she took that risk. But all the sales in the world, all the accolades, can never replace authenticity, which achieves the highest art. And that is why I believe someday, some way, her work and that of others who have spoken from the hearts of, and not down to, their subjects will endure and define us, long after that microscope has become unfashionable.

STEVE SCHNEIBLE

The Old Guard of the American Summer

"Northeastern Pennsylvania is the summer camp capital of the world," says Pike county judge Alan Cooper. It's another staff meeting as part of camp prep at Camp Oneka. The counselors are rapt with attention in their gleaming white staff polo shirts and dark navy skirts; the scene is reminiscent of some unpainted Norman Rockwell still, or maybe a vaguely WWII propaganda poster, with all these straight uniformed shoulders sitting in line surrounded by the wood-paneled walls of the boat house. Judge Alan Cooper continues his spiel; he's a charming man, with the folksy affectations of a rural American who speaks with eloquence and authority. The judge has come to our small camp to give the boilerplate child and counselor protection rundown, which gets mildly uncomfortable. I'm leaning against the wall, next to my boss, Kevin, the co-owner and director of the camp. I've heard the speech once already, and Kevin has heard it God knows how many times, so we're respectfully half-listening. "Since some of the, um, unfortunate occurrences at a large school here in Pennsylvania," the judge continues, "the state has required that all employees who work with children be designated mandated reporters." My boss elbows and grins at me. "Hey, PSU! That's where you're going," he whispers. I smile wanly. "Yep," I reply, through thin lips.

Kevin sometimes makes me uncomfortable. He means well, and he's a good boss, but we just don't click. Ordinarily, that's not an issue or even all that uncommon in boss-employee relationships, but Kevin and I find ourselves pushed together quite a bit: we're the only men here. Camp Oneka is an all-girls' camp, marketed as a supportive asylum of leadership, camaraderie, and childhood fun to the East Coast's urbane country club families, most of whom live in Philadelphia, Manhattan, or Connecticut[2]. Kevin is here because he bought the camp with his wife, Becky, also co-director, from his parents-in-law, Dale and Barb Dohner, a retired high school teacher and nurse, respectively. I am here because Kevin needs to hire a male maintenance assistant every summer, and I happened to be a cheap local option. I always knew about Camp Oneka; the relatively small, fenced-off property sits on Fairview Lake, the lake whereupon my family's slipshod summer cabin has stood for over fifty years. You can't miss Camp from any position along the roughly three miles of Fairview's coast; in the twenty-first century's real estate market, Camp Oneka is the only sizable portion of the waterfront not dominated by houses. As a child, I could hear the cheers of competition from across the water while I sat on my parents' dock, and my father would regale me occasionally with tales of his own boyhood mischief with the camp, most notably the time he and a friend had tried to sneak a nighttime cruise with the senior girls, which ended in a midnight cacophony involving spotlights and a megaphone-amplified director's shouted threats. I never gave Camp Oneka much thought, though. I was busy as a self-indulgent kid, swimming and fishing on the azure waters of Fairview Lake or walking through the surrounding woods, dominated by American Beech and rhododendron and dappled with lichen-crusted Hemlock. By chance one summer, I ran into Becky at the coffee shop some miles away in the nearest town and essentially walked into a job.

I work as a professional wallflower, irrelevant to the camp's goings-on while I'm washing this, screwing in that, or, when the grim need arises, plunging toilets. Camp Oneka never stops—not for staff, not for the kids, not even for the parents on moving days, in which our sun-deadened multipurpose field is overrun with the Range Rovers and Cadillac Escalades of stockbrokers, doctors, and the garishly vogue middle-aged mothers who all sport Lululemon and, disconcertingly, speak with the same intonation and vernacular as their preteen and teenage daughters.

2 There's an eerie, elite aspect to some of these families. The parents are often attractive and successful, and there exists a small subpopulation of girls here who attend live-away boarding school for nine months of the year and Oneka for two more. Very few of these people tip; those that do tend to drive the more modest vehicles.

Summer camps have a perpetual motion to them that, as a camper, you take for granted: all is awash in leaf-diffracted sunlight and a breeze that ineffably appears to alleviate your sweat from soccer or canoeing. When working at camp as a man of constant background, I see and hear what makes summer camp the thing to which children look forward without knowing why it's so much fun. Our counselors work what are, in practice, 24-hour days, serving as stand-in mothers for the youngest kids and acting as hip guidance for the older ones, all in between running activities, managing drama[3], and adhering to the baroque schedule. The staff love their jobs; most have been coming back for several years, and many of those are former campers. Summer camps often have their own deliberately hackneyed traditions and legends, which make for great fireside fun and camp cohesion, but at Oneka, everyone genuinely believes in the "Oneka Spirit." When adults write the fairy tales that delight the young campers and bring nostalgia to the slightly older, the mantles of maturity and worldliness drift away with the campfire smoke: youthfulness seems one with the land, as generation after generation remembers the lakeside glow of embers as a sanctuary of innocence.

Six days a week, I roll into work and park my bicycle next to the rock climbing wall that stands out as unusually nice for the camp's facilities. The property has had many owners during its one-hundred-plus years on Fairview Lake, and the age shows: ancient signposts painted over dozens of times stand beside brand-new kayaks on the waterfront; a basketball/volleyball hybrid court is so dimpled with prolonged play that it is rendered useless on rainy mornings; and our five-year-old Dining Hall, above which are housed apartments and offices for the camp's administrative brass, is about twenty feet away from The Lodge, our most central and nostalgia-laden structure, a building so old that my daily sweepings feel Sisyphean against the perseverance of the perpetually dusty floorboards.[4] Many of the facilities are in minor states of disrepair,

---

3 Dale and I are both Eagle Scouts and were active Boy Scouts when we were young, which involved, of course, summer camp—but Boy Scout Summer Camp, an experience marked by militaristic hierarchy, pulling-up-of-oneself-by-one's-bootstraps rhetoric, and crudely boyish horseplay. As Dale says of the environments at boys' and girls' camps, "Boys hit each other and pee on things. Girls are smart and mean."

4 It is worth noting that The Lodge is practically begging for a fire. Without exaggeration, the only materials used in construction were stone, iron nails, and dangerous amounts of brittle lumber, and the shoddy stage at its front is equipped with antique, obscenely high-wattage stage lights that, when in use, produce a ten degrees Fahrenheit temperature delta between the stage and the house.

beyond the abilities of yours truly but not significantly enough to impact anything. Camp Oneka is content in itself, though, despite its hefty price tag. In the mountains of northeastern Pennsylvania, beyond the reaches of high-class parents, rickety appearances take on a quality of timelessness, slipping into the summer green.

The kids love the sun. It shines down promises of games and trips and sailing, of enjoyable swimming and, later, a pleasantly warm summer evening. I like the sun, too; when I'm down in the empty rows[5] working alone, I can look out on the lake and enviously watch the watersporting vacationers. I can look at my parents' house and watch the sunlight skitter across the wave-cut surface of the lake onto the quiet shoreline of the hamlet that is my workplace. In these moments of isolation, I get generally sentimental and reflective; I think about growing up on the lake during the summers of my own youth, of how lucky I was to have been a part of a community in an area in which these girls will always be seen as outsiders. The Fairview Lake Association and its members often refer to Oneka simply as "The Camp," and the Oneka sailors who compete in the Saturday sailboat races are universally held in contempt for their inexperience, incompetence, and general audacity for not taking sailing with the level of vindictive seriousness preferred by the stodgy FLA old guard. These girls come from families of not-insignificant money, but at Oneka, upper-class affectations melt away with the swells of camp songs, arts and crafts, and sporting events. I can hear the cheers[6] and screams of the Red v. White competitions, age-old Oneka traditions wherein the campers of each team forget their friendships for an hour as the red blood of rivalry begins to boil. The girls live for Red v. White. Each and every camper is assigned to a team her first year and competes with her comrades for team dominance each year thereafter; generally, Whites are selected for being cool and reserved, and Reds are selected for extroverted competitiveness, but legacy plays a large part in both team assignment and, subsequently, team devotion: if your mother was a Red, then you

5 "Row" is the camp terminology for the age-based living assignments. Juniors live in Junior Row and Intermediates live in Int Row, both of which use cabins for housing. Seniors live in the tent-based Senior Row, which is by far the nicest, nestled in the densest pines of the Camp and settled on the lakefront so as to catch the majority of the afternoon sun through the needles' canopy.

6 Embarrassingly, I once made an attempt to get the team captains to change the "1,2,3,4 who are we for?" chant to "6,5,4,3, for whom are we?" I was, deservedly, ignored.

are a Red. Hardly surprisingly, the deliberately fostered environment of high competitive stakes leads to intense emotional consequences. After the passions of the field, regardless of who wins, there's crying and hugging across both sides. Staff can't root for the teams officially, but I smile when I hear the Whites doing well; the Reds strike me as brash.

Camp Oneka feels like most a part of the lake when it rains. Rain at Fairview Lake is a special thing. Without warning, the standard western wind may shift and begin to shriek in uncoordinated bursts, darkening the water with pulses of erratic air. Monolithic clouds will roll over the horizon with a grim purpose, as waves turn gunmetal gray and trees tremble. Storms at Oneka are quite the natural interlude from standard summer camp fun, but the rain that brings the Camp closest together is the slow, unhurried rain of melancholically steady dreariness. During these times, the woods spring to a murky new life, as greens become mesmerizingly vibrant in the darkness of the cloud-covered wood; the smells of lake water, rotting timber, and wet underbrush fill the air with a heady aroma of a fresh sleepiness all around the lake. At the rain-hushed camp, I sit, reveling in the slowness, while counselors put on their best entertaining faces to keep the kids content during inside activities. Laughter and shrieks are still heard, but they now come from the overwarm buildings and are marked by the slightly solemn intimacy of uniting in spite of the weather. Camp Oneka feels empty in the rain. The quiet, imperturbable woods creep into our fenced-off acreage with the hazy stillness; look too long at the forlorn cabins and you realize that the only vanguard against decay into nature-overrun ruin is the kids who still beg their parents to send them here, that they may give youthful life to the outposts on the shore.

I hope that Oneka continues. Kevin and Becky work against a changing tide of what it means to be a kid of means in America. Many of these girls have friends from their private schools who cannot go to summer camp: there are leadership seminars to attend and highly competitive club sports for which weekly travel is a necessity. Scholarships and resumes dominate the talk of the most senior campers, and college looms over their heads in a pallor of parental and social class expectation. Camp Oneka's true safeguard against irrelevance lies in the innocent enthusiasm of the younger campers, in the corny traditions made anew to the coming generations and preserved religiously by the older.

Cold rain continues to fall lazily. Tonight, after I go home to a solitary dinner and *Seinfeld* not a half mile away, there will be storytelling and singing by the glow of flashlights, until the girls are lulled to sleep by the audible shimmer of drizzling on Fairview Lake. I'm an adult now, already falling prey to cynicism; I cannot help Camp even as a maintenance worker, for the woods and the mist have already taken me, calling me into the unknown, Adult world to make mistakes and learn hard lessons. But the children still play. Summers end. Best to enjoy them like kids at Camp.

NICK STANOVICK

My Father Turns Sixty Today

though I cannot reach him.

He is alive, with my sister, hiking the backcountry in Utah. I am in our valley, on our farm in the Pocono Mountains, the small town of Saylorsburg where I did my growing, where I felt my deepest pain.

To be severed from them is a peculiar, chilling feeling. I am performing his loneliness, house sitting for the first week of August, where the plush green reaches its crescendo, where dragonflies land on the pages I read.

The house has two years left before my father retires and it's sold to the highest bidder. I'm heartbroken. I tell my sister about this on our drive from Hudson, New York back to Brooklyn, where we live our siren lives. She is matter of fact. I wonder how we could have such different responses to the house we grew up in, the living room that held our mother's last breath, the pond and the rolling valley fields, the backroads traced behind our eyes.

I am never in the house alone. It is my place to retreat, to reconvene with my father, my family. And for the first time, I see my father's life more plainly: the plants are watered on Wednesday, the fish are fed at dusk, the dog is dying but needs to be fed, needs a loud clap to wake from the tiers of sleep he's earned from twelve years of sprinting the edges of the field. The house's interior is dilapidating, filth in the corners and flies on the sills. No touches of warmth, just the aged smell of living.

The outside retains its beauty, my father makes it so. At the pond, I sit between two skies, as the swallows missile and flit. The flowers make purple towers in their beds and the corn is taller than I am, two weeks from gifting their seed. I build my own fire, from twigs, to split wood, to the heavy logs my father cut himself. As the day ends, I'm placed inside a pinking lantern, the fire acting as a tiny wick. There is too much beauty to behold, to make language of. And there is no one to share it with. A phenomenon I haven't fully considered. I am never in the house alone, though my father is, always.

I pull brush from piles he has made around the farm. I put my hands into his gloves. My hands, already his, now his again. Thorned and bleeding, I feel the hot sun, and my heavy breath reminds me how working the land comes with sacrifice, how the city has changed me, thinned my skin into paper—easily burned, predictably plain. The cloudboats stroll across their skysea. In the yard, the bones of my father's favorite trout, picked clean. My eyes rememory the landscape: I am sixteen, pushing the mower, my mother bends to pick weeds from her flower bed, my father fastens to his wheelbarrow and my sister runs circles around the dog until he dizzies and falls. How many deaths can you count? How many still to come?

By her flowerbed the bees work their honey magic and the sunflower's neck begins to break. Slowly, in my bedroom, I stand in front of photos of me and my mother in Yellowstone, my parents at a wedding. Each picture is blurry and it suits them, the sharpness lost and dulled.

That everlasting question: is home a place or a people? I've been fixating on the loss of this place, but never considered how it would hollow without my father's presence. It is unbearable, a cathedral without its light, without its song. These small, ephemeral beauties—on the hill, whitetail deer bathed golden; along the bank, the heron's spear and slender; in the dark, the peepers pulse and pulse. Each evening my father sits in his iron chair, takes in what is his, and has no one to hold it with him, no shared memory by which to save it to. And as I sit here, in his iron chair, the water now a pool of night, I do not want it. There is too much to hold here with just two hands. *Happy birthday*, I say to the dark. *Happy birthday, happy birthday*, and the nightnoise peaks, and I am undone beneath starshine.

ELIZABETH TUSSEY

On Tussey Mountain

Twenty-three days after my mother died and a few days before the second anniversary of my father's death, I left the flatlands of Northeast Ohio for Alexandria, Pennsylvania - a borough nestled near the ridges of Tussey Mountain and along the Juniata River. I booked a room at The Edgewater Inn, a historic property built in 1767 by a descendant of William Penn. My primary aim for this trip was to conduct genealogy research in some of the courthouses and genealogy libraries in Blair and Huntingdon Counties; in reality, I was evading my fresh grief by immersing myself in a distant ancestral home.

When my father died after a brief but harrowing bout of lung cancer and liver failure in January of 2015, my widowed mother never had a chance to emerge from the ether of her grief. She followed him after a diagnosis of the same cancer on Christmas Day of 2016. Both of my parents were students at Kent State University during that fatal weekend of May 1970.

On May 2, 1970, the Governor of Ohio, James Rhodes, ordered The Ohio National Guard to leave their posts at an on-going trucker strike and assemble on the campus of Kent State University, where students and other civilians were protesting President Nixon's expansion of the Vietnam War into Cambodia. By the morning of Monday, May 4, after a weekend of increasing chaos on campus, both of my parents were terrified and hoping to return home as soon as their finals were finished. My father had a geography exam that afternoon, and on his way to Bowman Hall, he stopped near Taylor Hall and watched the interactions between the student protestors and guardsmen. Fifteen minutes after he left, the National Guard turned and fired upon the unarmed crowd. Even fifty years later, the reasons behind the shooting remain shrouded in mystery and controversy. The volley of gunfire killed four Kent State students and wounded nine more.

My mother was standing in line at the student credit union to get money for a ride home when the shots were fired. On the other side of campus, my father entered Bowman Hall. He heard a rush of footsteps as students burst into the building, seeking shelter from the gunfire erupting on a hill near Taylor Hall. My mother reached the teller window just as news as the shooting reached the college administration. Before my mother could receive her cash, the teller told her, "There's been a shooting. Campus is closed." She shut the window in my mother's face. My mother left the credit union and eventually located my father in the chaotic aftermath of the shooting.

My father decided to hitchhike to the Akron-Canton Airport in hopes of catching a flight back to Pittsburgh. A young woman with a newborn baby picked him up near downtown Kent. She told him that state troopers were pulling people out of cars for questioning on the way out of town. When a trooper actually did stop the car he was traveling in, my father hid under a pile of baby blankets in her backseat. He arrived to the Akron-Canton Airport and was able to book a flight back to Pittsburgh. While waiting for his flight, a kind stranger approached him and offered to call his mother to let her know he was okay. When my grandmother received this phone call, the man simply said, "There's been a shooting but your son is fine" before hanging up. My father's older brother, my Uncle John, was a Marine stationed in Da Nang, Vietnam, when the shooting happened. My grandmother immediately thought this bizarre phone call had to do with her enlisted son and not the son she believed to be safe at Kent State. Any time my Uncle John recounts this story, he always points out that his civilian brother saw more combat and was shot at more than he was during his tour in Vietnam.

My parents' shared trauma from the events of May 4, 1970, would mean a lifetime of mental and physical illnesses. I've often heard the phrase, "my parents did the best they could" in recovery communities. This sentiment was true of my mother and father; they were wonderful parents despite the horrors they lived with and the behavior that comes with unresolved trauma. My father retired from American Standard when he was sixty-five and died just eight months later. My mother, who was a year older than my father, died when she was sixty-eight. I was their only child and my mother's death was the denouement to the near-unbearable realization of my worst fears.

They drafted their wills when they were in their early fifties. Did this do because they knew the toll their lifestyles were sure to take? Did they simply want to get such a morbid task out of the way before it started to become a reality? Or did they know all too well how quickly and senselessly a life could end? Despite their forethought and planning, I still faced the reality of responsibilities left in the wake of sudden, untimely deaths—including the seemingly intractable task of cleaning out, repairing, and selling my barely functional childhood home.

During the final weeks of my mother's illness, I began to feel a pull to the mountains. When the French drains in the house overflowed and flooded the basement the week before my mother died, I pictured the hush of snow-covered hemlocks along the curving roads of Huntingdon County to calm my panic as I faced back-to-back calls with the plumbers and my mother's hospice nurse. After she passed, the same image would emerge from the fog of my insomnia, as I lay awake waiting to hear a voice that was forever stilled.

My father's stories about his ancestors, an assortment of misfits and exiles from Scotland, Northern Ireland, and Finland, instigated my fascination with the Ridge-and-Valley Appalachians. One story involved the murder of an eighteenth-century midwife on Tussey Mountain while on her way to deliver a baby. Supposedly the mountain was named in memory of this ill-fated woman. While the Tussey Mountain Ski Resort in State College is probably the most familiar association Central Pennsylvanians have with my surname, the name actually applies to an entire mountain range. Tussey Mountain begins as far north as Tusseyville near State College and extends over eighty miles south into Maryland.

I first visited my geographic namesake during our yearly drives across the state of Pennsylvania. Like many working-class families in Northeastern Ohio and Western Pennsylvania, my family vacations took place in Ocean City, Maryland, rather than the pricier Outer Banks of North Carolina. Some of my earliest memories are of car rides along the Pennsylvania Turnpike. My father always stopped at the Breezewood Exit as a halfway point on our journey to Maryland. In recent years, I've seen a photograph of Breezewood make the rounds on various social media platforms. The picture features a chaotic mess of fast-food signs, gas stations, cars, and pitted asphalt. The image serves as a bit of infrastructural critique depending on the context in which it is posted—often to decry the lack of walkable streets and general decay of American civic life. For me, Breezewood was my first view of Tussey Mountain and is connected to my conception of my ancestors' rural lives, despite the commercialized wasteland Breezewood signifies. Breezewood also served as a trigger for my father's stories. They were welcome distractions during those long drives and took me away from the chaotic present of my childhood—worries over the stability of my father's job as a millwright at American Standard, my mother's all-consuming anxiety—and into a distant but enthralling past. His stories were distorted as family legends often are, embroidered and altered on their way from mouth to mouth, generation to generation. By the time they reached my father they were amalgamations of truth and fancy. Even the origins of our last name are so obscured by fable that, twenty years after I began researching our origins, I have yet to confidently pinpoint the source of our name.

I have searched for other Tusseys during my travels—flipping through a phonebook in a hotel in Glasgow to the T section and finding nothing. Tussey is a name of American origin; the surname does not exist in strong numbers in any other country I've searched. Despite the vaguely Gaelic sound and spelling of the name, no Scottish or Irish tourist shops sell mugs featuring a Tussey tartan. Even online family arms websites struggle to place the name—some claim it to be of German origin; others give it a French bent and suggest the modern spelling is a derivative of Tusseux. When my father would tell the story of my murdered ancestress and her mountain monument, her first name was lost—only the aim of her journey, her foul end and her surname carried through the centuries and to a lovely ridge among the Appalachian Mountains. When I lost my father, I lost the living link to this past. I've been interested in genealogy research since I was a teenager, and my father's passing encouraged me to chase various details of his stories with greater focus until a clearer picture of my ancestors emerged.

After a year or two of intense research, I learned that Tussey Mountain was named after a woman who shares my first and last name: Elizabeth Tussey. My father had no firm knowledge of her story when he named me but I am thrilled to have something in common with her. The eighteenth-century Elizabeth Tussey was not murdered but was most likely widowed when her husband was killed during a skirmish along the Pennsylvania and Maryland border in 1757. A man named John McCullough recorded the vague reference to the death of this unnamed male Tussey in his diary. The diary entry details the massacre of a Major Campbell and his men in one of many violent encounters between the French and their Native American allies, parts of the British army, and settler militias during The Seven Years War.

Various accounts of my ancestress' life can be found in old newspapers and county history books and, while these tales are warped by colonizer narrative tropes and the passing of centuries, some details remain the same among the various sources I've uncovered. Elizabeth left Philadelphia following her husband's death and made her journey west with two small sons: John (my direct ancestor) and his younger brother, Jacob. She was a camp follower in the company of Colonel Burd during the development of what would later become Forbes Road. She settled near the current town of Everett, Pennsylvania, and became an alewife, traded pack horses with the Lenape tribe, and eventually built her own tavern. Elizabeth was possibly a sex worker and eventually made enough money to establish her own tavern north of the Juniata River near Lower Snake Spring. Her son John moved north along the mountain named after his mother and eventually settled in Alexandria. This branch of the Tussey family flourished along the border of Blair County and Huntingdon County. John Tussey's son, David, and his wife Elizabeth had fifteen children who married into the Scottish families living in what was once called "Scotch Valley" due to their ubiquity in the region. The lives of my Stewart, Dean, Crawford, and Moore ancestors were equally as fascinating and I began to find bits of truth in my father's legends. He died before I was able to share most of these stories with him. However, in the act of following the clues he left in his stories, I felt as close to him as I could ever hope to be again.

Following my mother's death, I found that my homing instincts to return to Tussey Mountain were fruitful. During those first trips to Central Pennsylvania, I noticed the churning of grief seemed to slow when I'd hit the long stretch of Route 22 east of Pittsburgh and rise over the first crest of the Laurel Highlands. Edgewater Inn became the perfect base of operations for the series of trips I took in 2017 for both logistical and emotional reasons. Located right off of the highway, the inn was central to Hollidaysburg, Williamsburg, Alexandria, and Huntingdon where multiple generations of my ancestors lived all those centuries ago. Edgewater Inn did not have reliable internet and I would be forced to sit with my grief rather than engaging in my habit of staying up all night scrolling through my phone. I often walked out to the main room of the inn in the dead of night and sat next to the snuffed fireplace that was built during my ancestors' lifetimes. My thoughts would traverse the centuries, from the eighteenth-century trials of my ancestress Elizabeth Tussey to the fresh loss of my parents, and forward to whatever future the trajectory of my own life held in store.

In the mornings, I would take long drives out to various sites of my own family history and local libraries and courthouses. The healing effect these rural excursions had on me was most notable when I would interact with strangers during my visits. I had developed strange and embarrassing habits in the months following my mother's death, most notably in my speech. I taught college courses for a decade prior to the death of my parents and prided myself on the clarity and confidence I maintained before the crowd of sleepy undergraduates in my morning courses. I quit teaching when my father died, partly due to the rapid decline in my speaking abilities. These issues only worsened following my mother's death. While speaking, I would lose words mid-sentence and stutter out a non-sensical mixture of words and extraneous noises. Eventually the only person I felt comfortable speaking to was my partner, Cooper.

After my first trip out to Tussey Mountain, I realized that these speech issues seemingly vanished when I was in my ancestral home. In the mornings, I would take long drives out to various sites of my own family history and local libraries and courthouses. The healing effect these rural excursions had on me was most notable when I would interact with strangers during my visits. I could speak confidently and at length about my research with anyone who asked. I even hosted a talk on my research at a local genealogical society without a single incident. I'm not sure if the issues went away because I was physically distant from the setting for so many recent sorrows, or if my attempts to immerse myself in the past provided a similar temporal distance from the deaths of my parents. My speech issues almost always resumed when I returned to the heap of responsibilities waiting for me in Ohio, but with less and less intensity after each trip I took.

Hollidaysburg, the hometown of my Moore ancestors, became one of my favorite stopping points during these research trips. I did not mind traveling alone and would sit at a dining room table at the US Hotel Tavern gastropub, sipping on beer and eavesdropping on ghost stories about the lovely, old building. I enjoyed chatting with my favorite waitress there, who often gifted me with a free sample of dessert on my way out the door. I never leave Hollidaysburg without a visit to the Presbyterian Cemetery. The drive to the cemetery from the US Hotel and Tavern is a steep climb up one of the tallest hills in Hollidaysburg. Although I've been there many times, I'm always stunned by the view. When I visit, one of my favorite places for contemplation is in the older part of the cemetery. A large boulder marks the location of the original church before it burned in the early 1800s. The tombstones lean every which way in this section and even the towering obelisks bow towards the downward creep of the hillside. One particularly crooked row is comprised of five generations of my ancestors. The inscriptions on these stones are faded but still readable. I run my hands over their familiar names and try to make out the short quotations inscribed on some of their stones. Most of these words are lost, and with them sentiments I can never uncover. I no longer despair over the unknowable.

Long before my ancestors lived and died, the Ridge-and-Valley Appalachians towered above the valleys and the ancient rivers that still wind their way through Central Pennsylvania. When I stand on the worn and windy bluff where my ancestors rest, or drive the roads that curve around the mountain that bears my name, I can feel time passing through me. Time erodes my grief and wears me down and brings me closer to these faded names on these crooked stones. If we go anywhere when we die, I know I will return to these mountains.

JERRY WEMPLE

The True and Complete Story of Orange

It is the second week of July and I am sitting on Chuck's wooden front porch steps. I'd been in town a week. I see her. She is across the street, sitting on the cement steps of her front porch. She is the cutest girl I have ever seen: petite, long blonde hair, and wearing an expression that mesmerizes. She has on jeans and an orange t-shirt. Her favorite color, I learn later, is orange. I watch her for a few minutes. She is troubled. She is holding her hand in a funny way. Sometimes she frowns, looks like she is trying to figure out something. I am not sure why I do it, what it is that propels me across the street and to her side.

What I say now is true and it is not true. Nothing is ever true, because there is always more than one truth And nothing is ever complete because there is never an end. Here is how I know:

Long ago, in a different time and a different place, but really yesterday and in a town twenty miles from here, I was sixteen and it was July, and I had just returned to the town after living in Florida. The town was a small town. A set of railroad tracks ran the length of the town. Sometimes you had to wait ten minutes, until the long line of rocking railcars ended, to continue your walk. Sometimes a guy would be standing on the platform at the back of the caboose, and he would wave back. Like most river towns of the region, the streets were laid out in a grid. Front Street ran parallel to the river. Market Street ran perpendicular to Front Street, bisecting the town. There were a few places near the creek which forms the southern border of the town where the streets grow crowded and irregular. Mostly they were in a grid. The people of the town had always been practical, liked order. After all, the town was built on the site of a fort, put there to keep the brown-skin Indigenous people away in the wilderness. There is a gray wall, twenty-feet high in places, running the length of Front Street. It was built in the 1940s to hold back the flood waters. Sometimes it holds things in. At the north end of town, if you peer over the wall, you can see the confluence of the two branches of the river. The river is expansive there, over a half mile wide. It looks like nothing, not even a tall gray wall, might restrain it.

There was a highway across the river and late at night you could hear the semi-trucks gearing up or down depending on whether they were going north and making the hill toward Winfield or headed east or curving in between the rocky cliff face of Blue Hill and the river to cross a bridge over its west branch in another two miles. I loved the night sounds of the town: the trucks echoing across the river, the warning dings of train crossing gates and then the heavy groan of diesel locomotives pulling fifty or sixty cars, a quiet walk down alleys with the only sound the faint muddled noise of a television coming from someone's front room.

I was sixteen and hadn't lived in this town for six and a half years. I left in fourth grade, a few weeks before Christmas. I came up every summer for two weeks, when my mother and stepfather took vacation. Two years before I stayed the whole summer. I stayed at my grandmother's. I stayed over at Chuck's as much as I could. Chuck was less than a year younger than me. He would have been my best friend, except I only got to see him those two vacation weeks each year. That summer, his mother worked out of town all day and paid us little mind during the evening. His stepdad was a long-haul trucker often gone a week or more at a time.

We took his stepdad's rifles out, walking the alleys until we got out in the woods along Kirshner's Hill. Mostly we took .22s, but once we took the 7mm Remington Magnum rifle. It sounded like thunder ripping open a sunny summer sky. We also took Chuck's stepdad's motorcycles out. He had a purple Honda 305 Scrambler and a 250cc Yamaha Enduro with a blue tank. The Scrambler was a good road bike with a lot of pop for its size. The Enduro was a knobby-tired dirt bike with a headlight to make it street legal.

Once we rode to other side of the river, past the truckers and up Blue Hill, to some girl's house. It was raining and I was gunning the Enduro down County Line Road. The road had a steep decline and I was sure

I was not going to make the curve and I would go off the road and fly down the cliff until I hit one of the broad oak trees on the side of the hill. My mind was clear and I was ready to die. I was fourteen. The bike made the curve and I geared down.

The next summer, I didn't come up to Pennsylvania at all. I stayed behind in Florida because our vacation was in late August, overlapping with the start of school, and I wanted to try out for football. I stayed with the neighbors across the street, Jerry and Nancy. They were poor and lived in a trailer and had three kids. I brought my stereo over to their house and listened to Jim Croce tapes. At night, Jerry and I and some of the other guys from the neighborhood went snook fishing off the Pine Island Bridge in Matlacha. I made the football team and went to practice twice a day. I did not like football. I lacked the blind aggression needed to play. The team lost every game.

The summer I was sixteen I was back in Pennsylvania. My mother was divorcing my stepdad, which was okay by me. I hated him. He had a crew cut and a fat face with jowls like Richard Nixon. He ate runny eggs with mustard on them. In May, my mother headed north, for what she said was going to be a temporary visit. Only that wasn't true. We'd been in Florida nearly seven years by then. In the fall, I'd be a junior in high school. I figured my stepfather would move to some trash trailer down the road after my mother came back. But mid-summer I was the one who had moved.

I finished my school year. This girl who lived in a neighborhood about a mile away was interested in me. Her name was Noel, like Christmas. At night I would walk over there, and we would hang out. Noel was nearly as tall as me and had brown hair and brown eyes. She was on the track team and was strong and fast. Mostly we walked around. I don't think we held hands much. We just walked and talked. Then I walked home. Once we were sitting on her couch and we started kissing, and then her older brother came in and told us we were too young for that kind of stuff.

That summer I tried to get a job. I had a driver's license, but I did not have a car and there were no businesses within walking distance. I went to summer school instead, walking the two miles to school to take gym so I would not have to take it during the school year and could take an elective like newspaper writing. Then my mother sent a plane ticket and I returned to Pennsylvania. While I was living in Florida alone with my stepfather, we did not do anything together. Once the regular school year ended, he gave me these parameters: "I don't care how late you stay out, just don't come home with the cops." I was an Eagle Scout, went fishing, and was a bit of a shy kid who liked school. My stepfather's only recreation was drinking a case of beer by himself each weekend.

It is the second week of July. I am sitting on the cement steps of Chuck's front porch. My skin is deep copper, its summer color. My hair is a collaboration of dark curls. No one in this town looks like me. No one in my family looks like me. I do not fit in here. I do. In this town of German and English names, my own family contained names like Shultz, and Haas, and Bauman. Though I was adopted, I had found out, two years before—the summer of rifles and motorcycles—that I was also blood kin. Chuck's mom had also given birth to me, the result of her affair with a black man in Baltimore. My mother, who I then learned is by blood my aunt, adopted me from the Scranton orphanage where I'd been left. She raised me as her own. Chuck's trucker stepdad, drunk, told us this one night.

I had gone to St. Michael's school until it was almost Christmas in fourth grade. In second grade I played the robot in the play *The Thumpity Bumpity Box*. We put on the play on a small wooden stage in the basement parish hall. My mom made my costume out of boxes she got from the supermarket, and silver spray paint, and Magic Markers. In my first communion picture taken that same spring, I am marching in a line of eight-year-olds in white robes, hands folded as if in prayer. I am easy to pick out.

Even before I reach school age, I am keenly aware I do not look like I belong in this town, that I am an oddity. There were few people of color in the region when I was growing up. Sometimes I would see a Black person on TV and recognize a kind of connection. Still, to a kid, television—a place of cartoons, game shows, and soap operas—is a distant magic. It doesn't walk the streets of the town.

As I sat there that day looking at the girl across the street, I knew where I was. There was some level of familiarity and belonging. I had relatives in the neighborhood, on farms outside of town. My half-sister lived next door with her two kids, the twins. My grandmother used to live there. I have a picture taken when I was seven and I am standing on that front porch. I am dressed in a blue suit with a red and blue striped bow tie and an ill-fitting fedora. A few minutes after the picture was taken, I was on my way to Easter Sunday Mass at St. Michael's.

Walking across the street and setting next to that girl is one of the great moments of my life. A few weeks before, I would not have done it. In Florida, I would not approach the cutest girl I ever saw, sit down next to her, and hold her hand. That's what I do with Orange. Her thumb and forefinger are stuck together with Krazy Glue. I hold her hand and roll her finger and thumb around with mine. The bond is not hard to break. After five minutes, we go for a walk.

We walked a lot that summer. We walked up to the hill section of town to Cindy's house. Cindy lived in a big brick house with an enclosed porch and was Orange's best friend. Late at night, after Orange is home, and I should be, I go for walks all over town. One night, when the air is thick with August's humidity and fog, I walk the black bridge. Trains stopped running on it years before, and in a few years it will be torn down, leaving only the stone pilings as a reminder of what once was. That night I walk slowly to the center of the bridge. A thick fog has settled into the moonless night. I can hear the water below, can barely make out its shifting shape through the timbers of the bridge deck. I can hear the trucks on the west shore. To my right, I hear the noises of the town: cars driving slow down alleys, the whine of industrial compressors, somebody yelling for somebody else to get the hell back here now. The confluence of the river is a mile to my north. I cannot see it. I hear two people walking, coming toward me. I walk toward them. We meet. It's just two stoners catching a buzz.

Even though I had a driver's license I had no car. The only time I got to use the car was to go to the job my cousin Wendy got me at the Arthur Treacher's Fish & Chips fast-food place that just opened across the river on the highway. The job wasn't as bad as it could have been. The twenty-something manager, Rick, was a decent guy. And I worked with Herbie a lot. He was a funny kid whose dad's main occupation seemed to be his afternoon "paperboy" route. I always wondered if Herbie was embarrassed that his dad was a paperboy. The town paper came out in the afternoon. Sometimes if you were walking around town right after school you could see Herbie's dad, the *Daily Item* bag with its safety-orange strap slung over his shoulder, chucking papers on porches. I didn't have a dad.

One morning, when we were opening up, Herbie blew himself across the room. The deep fryers were gas. Herbie bent down to light one of them, but turned the lever to "main" instead of "pilot." When he struck a match there was a sudden noise, a combination of whompf and bang, and Herbie was propelled ten feet across the floor. He sat, legs askew, against the brick back wall of the kitchen. His blond bangs and eyebrows and cheesy sparse mustache were singed, gone. I laughed for a long time. Rick came out from the back-room office and wigged.

One night I almost killed everyone: the manager, Herbie, and me. It was near closing and Rick asked me to mop the front area, out by the booths and the order counter. I was glad to do it. Most of our customers were older and came in early. We hadn't been busy for a long time. It was something to do other than counting the clicks of the time clock. I took to the task with thoroughness of those grateful to get a chance to prove themselves. What I thought I might prove at an off-brand fast food outlet in central Pennsylvania is beyond my recall. I was about halfway done when Rick came out of the office choking, eyes tearing. In an effort to get the greasy floor clean, I had used both ammonia and bleach in the mop water. This is a dangerous and potentially lethal combination. It makes chloramine gas, something close to what the Germans used in World War I. It took a long time for us to air out the restaurant. Some things do not mix.

Here is the thing: I will not use her name. Like the power that propelled me across the street to meet her, some un-nameable force now holds me back from renewing that familiarity. Respect? Regret? What is this queer feeling that lurks in between others? It sits on the edge of being and laughs. It knows what has been won and lost. Here is what I know: to her friends, she was known by one name. Her family called her another.

After Orange and I had been together a while, and I was spending most of my time with her, Chuck began to tease me. He kept singing the chorus to Elvin Bishop's "Fooled Around and Fell in Love," which was a popular song that summer. That fall, I would think about her and listen to the *Born to Run* album by Springsteen, sometimes stopping to replay "She's the One." Sometimes I would listen to David Bowie's version of "Sorrow" from his album *Pin Ups*.

With your long blonde hair and your eyes of blue
The only thing I ever got from you was sorrow

* * *

You never do what you know you oughta
Something tells me you're a devil's daughter

One night Orange and I are coming down from the hill section of town, heading toward our neighborhood. The night is getting cold. In Florida, I wore sandals a lot, mostly when I went out of the neighborhood. In my old neighborhood I often went barefoot. I am in Pennsylvania, still wearing my Florida sandals. We stop at my house. No one is home. My mother is two houses over, visiting her own mother. I kiss Orange once we are inside the heavy wooden door of my house. We kiss often. We are not like the sickening high school couples always lipped-locked to the mild disgust and envy of their friends. It is always in the shadows, away from others. It is between us. It is enough. Other times we hold hands and smile. Orange and I go upstairs, to my room. She sits on my bed. I put on socks and my white Adidas with green stripes and two pair of shoelaces, green and white. We leave. Just as we get outside my room, my mother starts up the steps to the second floor. I tell her I stopped to get some shoes, and that I am going to take Orange home, and then see what Chuck is doing. The next day, my mother tells me that I should not have girls up in my room at night when she is not home.

School started. I had homeroom with Mr. Lee. It was rumored that his wife made his suits out of old drapes. By the looks of it the rumors were true. He had on something purple and patterned and oddly corduroy-looking. My actual classes were good and interesting. Except for speech, the last period of the day. The teacher was a benevolent racist. He coached basketball and bugged me every day to try out for the team. He never asked me if I could play. He never asked me if I liked to play, or if I was any good. After the season of football, I played soccer and was on the wrestling team in Florida. When I tried out for the team, he was disappointed. My cousin Jackie was in that class. She was tall and blonde and had a German last name.

Here is the best part about America: reinvention. By moving back to the town from Florida, I got to reinvent myself. The power of the plane ride I took was that it transformed me. For Orange, I was this guy who was both intentioned and thoughtful. I crossed the street, held her hand, helped her. In my new school, I was this kid who had lived in Florida, who knew Jamaican slang and about Bob Marley, who played soccer instead of football, who knew different stories and would listen to your old ones with new ears.

For the first couple of weeks of school many of my old classmates from St. Michael's came up and said hello. Most of the Catholic school kids went to the local public high school because there was no Catholic high school in town. The last time I saw them was fourth grade. Sometimes they would ask: "Didn't you used to be Arthur?" My real name is Arthur. At St. Michael's school, the nuns called me Arthur. Taught to bow to the authority of the Church, I never corrected them. Thus, for the most part, the kids at St. Michael's knew me as Arthur. Everyone in my family called me Jerry.

When school starts Orange no longer acknowledges me. She does not sit out on her porch anymore. She does not talk to me in school. I ask her friend Cindy. "She can't" is all that Cindy says. I press for an explanation. None is offered. What am I to think? Perhaps Orange is ashamed of me. Perhaps I do not fit in with her image in the school. Perhaps she cannot reinvent herself. She has always lived in this town. The school does not have a soccer team. I go to a few football games. I see her in the Bravettes, the flag twirler unit of the marching band.

By late September I need a coat. I have not owned a coat in years. I get one in October. I do have an orange sweater. I got it in late summer, when Orange and I were still together. I know she will like it, or at least appreciate the gesture. The sweater is really a Philadelphia Flyers jersey that I buy on sale at the sports store uptown. It is the only orange sweater I can find. That winter, Brian, who is a really cool kid, keeps asking me to play on his hockey team. I had just moved up from Florida. I cannot ice skate.

After I failed at the basketball tryout, my friend Dave said I should try out for wrestling, that he'd introduce me to the coaches and the team. Wrestling was big at this school, state champion big. My cousin Jesse, who is three or four years younger than me, was a runner-up in the state tournament. He got a four-year college scholarship out of it. I wasn't good, but it gave me something to do. Dave introduced me to Hope, the younger sister of his girlfriend. She was cute, aggressive. She had short brown hair and blue eyes. We spent a lot of time together. We went on actual dates. I drove her across the river to Pizza Hut and sat next to her in a big, red-vinyl booth. She told me she was cold. I offered her my jacket. She said that when she said "I'm cold" it really meant "Put your arm around my shoulder." Sometimes I went to her house and her parents were nice to me. They had an Irish Setter. I liked that dog. Sometimes we watched TV at her house with her parents and younger brother and sister. One week *Roots* was on. *Roots* was a television mini-series focused on African American history, much of it covering the period of slavery. There were scenes of whippings and humiliation, of escapes and captures. I watched most of one segment with them, then walked home. I did not go back to their house the rest of that week.

In March, a week after my birthday, Hope broke up with me. Her parents liked me well enough, but her grandmother, the school nurse, put pressure on Hope and her parents because she did not like her granddaughter dating a half-breed kid. Over the next year and few months until I graduated, I would occasionally visit the nurse's office. I would say I had a headache, take an aspirin that was offered, then sit in silence staring straight ahead until I felt it time to go.

When I was a senior and she was a junior, Hope got pregnant by her then boyfriend. He was a kid named Clyde who drove a beat up van and joined the Navy. Hope had the kid, finished school. A couple years later, Hope was at Cindy's wedding. She sat by herself, a row or two behind me. At the end of the service, I turned and we were face to face. Then we walked down the aisle and exited the church. We joined the same small group of friends on the sidewalk ten feet from the church steps. Someone said my name. Hope, a few feet away, smiled at me. She said she hadn't recognized me. I wondered how anyone could be such a liar.

Spring is prom season. I helped decorate the gym for the prom, but I didn't go. There was a girl who I worked with at the movie theater uptown who I liked. Despite my experiences, I might have asked her to the prom, but she had an older stoner boyfriend. On a Friday, when we were done with the decorations for Saturday's prom, my friend Scott, and the girl with the stoner boyfriend, and another girl who talked a lot, got into Scott's car to go to a party in a grove outside of town. I asked Scott to stop by the garage in the alley behind my house, just a block over from the school. I got out, grabbed a fifth of lime-flavored vodka stashed in the tall grass on the side of the building. On the ride out to the party no one wanted a drink of warm lime vodka. I drank it all.

The next year a girl named Sherry was talking to me after Mass outside of St. Michael's. She was talking about the upcoming prom in a hinting manner. Her mother was nearby. She shushed Sherry and pulled her away. Sherry probably thought her mother wanted to go home for dinner, but by now I had come to recognize the face of disdain. I watched Sherry's blonde hair disappear across the parking lot. The next Friday, a girl named Laurie actually asked me directly to the prom. I said okay. Then on Monday, she told me her father would not let her go with me. I forget the term she said he used, colored kid, or something like that.

Laurie and I saw each other off and on for a few years. We saw each other a lot. The thing is, we never went out in public because it is a small town, and she was afraid of word getting back to her father. The thing is, she never really gave up her other boyfriend, the one her father could accept. A couple of years out of high school, Laurie and I were seeing each other for a few months. She had her own apartment and a job at the hospital doing data entry on second shift. I was working a job out of town during the week and trying to figure out a viable means of escape, from that town, from my life. That fall and winter, I would meet Laurie at her place on Friday nights at 11:30. One Friday someone else answered the door. This girl said Laurie moved. I didn't ask where. Two summers later, I saw Laurie when I was pulling into the parking lot of the supermarket on North Fourth Street. She had a baby and was with her boyfriend. I parked the car, went into the store, and got what I needed.

On the night of the prom that I did not attend with Laurie, I walked up the hill to Ricky's house. Ricky played on the basketball team I did not play on. I drank a case of beer in his garage with him and a skinny guy with a blond Afro that everybody called Jetson. He was the drummer of a local rock band and the boyfriend of Ricky's sister. Everybody thought that band was cool because each summer they toured Canada. Sometimes they still play shows locally. Jetson asked me why I wasn't going to the prom. I told him I didn't like getting dressed up. He handed me another beer.

Nearly a year after Orange stopped talking to me, Orange returns. She asks me to meet her at the Spruce Street cemetery. We walk the gravel road that parallels the railroad tracks, out behind the wire rope plant and the supermarket chain warehouses. There is a creek just beyond the tree line. It's foul, polluted with sediment and poison runoff from an anthracite mine fifteen miles away and shut decades before. The stench water slogs its last half mile to the river.

Orange and I stand under the broad canopy of a maple tree. She puts her hands in my back pockets and her head on my chest. It may be the happiest I have ever been. It may be the happiest I have ever been because it is before I learn that no matter how happy you are, there is always more to the story. We meet there several times on through the summer. Sometimes we kiss, but not as much as before. Once a train passed by on the tracks about a hundred feet away. I wave to a man peering out the window of the engine. He only looks at us.

I would like to say that everything works out between us, Orange and me, but you know that isn't true. The truth is she never came back. Sure, we met those times, but I could tell. By then Orange had begun to hang out with Bob, a friend of Cindy's boyfriend. He was tall, good looking. That first summer we were together, I sometimes told her that I was going to buy an orange van, and I would wait the year until she graduated, and then we would drive to California, watch the sun slip like an orange ball into the ocean. She would smile and pretend to believe me. This time I told Orange the truth. She never blinked or denied it. She knew too. She would marry Bob right after high school. They moved two hours away to Maryland for his job as a welder. At least she got that far.

Not long after I moved back to the region, my friend Steve, who still lives in that town, was talking to me on the phone. We were talking about a bunch of stuff, mostly him telling bits and pieces about people we knew. Then he told me about Orange. She graduated in his class, a year behind me. I had lived out of the area for the most part since graduation and had only returned a few months before. He told me she was dead. She got cancer and died. He told me this just the way you might mention any person who you kind of remembered. Orange and me: he had forgotten. I wondered if everyone had. I wondered if one person had.

Sometimes I do not care about the town at all. Memories turn rancid like the dirty chemical water of the creek, and my heart turns cold against it. But I have always loved the river. It has power. Sometimes it is weak, and sometimes it is strong. But you cannot stop it. You can only try to understand it. Truth be told, I still love the town too: the big houses up on the hill and the smell of the fresh bread from the bakery, the train whistling and rocking down the tracks late at night, the corner store with Hershey's Fudjos in the cooler and big bottles of RC Cola in another. But that town is gone, disappeared like boats come off the river when the season is done.

Here is the last thing I know about Orange. Years later, after high school, but while she was still alive and living with Bob in Maryland, I ran into her brother Craig in a bar. I was in the Navy then, stationed in Virginia and came home on leave sometimes. It was not unusual to run into Craig. It was a small town and the places to go out were not numerous. A few times we spent a couple of hours shooting pool and drinking Rolling Rock. The bar was on North Fourth Street and was called The Bitter End. I had been going in there since my senior year of high school. Craig was three or four years older than me and worked at the garage door factory outside of town. He always seemed like a cool guy. He wasn't flashy or full of himself. His girlfriend Meryl was always by his side. He was easy going and would compliment you on a good pool shot like he meant it, even if it cost him the game. He gave good, practical advice. Once he told me how he saved all his bar change, putting it in a jar when he came home at night, and that it added up quickly. He told me I should do that, too, because there would be times I would be glad to have that money around. I did and I was.

That night the place was crowded and we quit playing pool for a while. We did a couple of shots of apple schnapps at the bar. I bought us two more. Then he told me. He told me how much his sister had liked me, and how she never wanted to break up with me or stop talking to me. He told me how their father beat her each time he knew she was with me. He said that she cried every night for months, but their father was relentless. She was not allowed to talk with me, at home, at school, anywhere. He'd not have a daughter of his going out with a colored kid. My head grew heavy and dull. I wondered what names the old man had used for me, for his own daughter. What kind of father would beat his petite, beautiful girl into submission? One that lived in that town, I guessed. I have pictures on my office wall of that town. One, a photograph I took from Blue Hill, the place of the motorcycle and oak tree. The picture shows the two branches of the river meeting at the town, merging, creating a new and powerful thing.

Sometimes people ask me if I like the town so much, now that I live in the region again, why I don't live in that town again. Sometimes I am still living there and then. Sometimes time does not exist. Sometimes time is a child in a Sunday suit and crooked hat thinking of church, and candy, and where he belongs. Sometimes time is a river washing everything away. Sometimes I think about Orange and know that she is still living somewhere in Maryland. I wish her well.

Acknowledgments

The following essays, some in slightly different versions, first appeared in the following journals:

- "Elements" by Charisse Baldoria—*Passengers Journal*
- "What the Old Ones Show Us" by Todd Davis—*Northern Woodlands Magazine*
- "A Rye Sense of Place" by Jimmy Guignard—*Mountain Home Magazine*
- "Centralia Mine Fire" by Leonard Kress—*Bad Penny Review*
- "Rooms" by Abby Minor—*Contrary Magazine*
- "The True and Complete Story of Orange" by Jerry Wemple—*Hamilton Stone Review*

Contributors

Charisse Baldoria is a classical pianist, composer, writer, and educator. Born in the Philippines, she came to the United States as a Fulbright scholar for graduate school in music. She has performed on five continents and is a music professor at Commonwealth-University-Bloomsburg. Her work has appeared in *CutBank, Windmill: The Hofstra Journal of Art & Literature, Passengers Journal, The Asian Pacific American Journal*, and others. Her writing has received support from *Kenyon Review*, VONA, and the DISQUIET International Literary Program. She was a 2023 DISQUIET Literary Prize finalist in nonfiction and was shortlisted for fiction in 2024.

Aurora Bonner is an environmentally inspired writer. A native Pennsylvanian, her writing focused on the complexities of living in rural America. Her work has been published through regional and national publications, including *Hippocampus Magazine*, *Under the Gum Tree*, *Assay: Journal of Nonfiction Studies*, the *Colorado Review* and elsewhere. She holds an MFA from Wilkes University.

David Allan Brooks has lived in Hughesville for the past forty years. He tends to make frequent and seemingly pointless forays into hills surrounding the valley where he lives. His work has appeared in *West Branch. Right Livelihood,* a chapbook of his poems was published by Pavement Saw. He has recent work in *The Phare* and *Maryland Literary Review.*

Grant Clauser's sixth poetry book, *Temporary Shelters*, is forthcoming from Cornerstone Press. His poems have appeared in *The American*

Poetry Review, Greensboro Review, Kenyon Review and other journals. He's an editor for a large media company and teaches poetry at Rosemont College.

Bill Conlogue teaches American literature at Marywood University. He is the author of *Here and There: Reading Pennsylvania's Working Landscapes* and *Undermined in Coal Country: On the Measures in a Working Land.*

Todd Davis is the author of seven books of poetry, most recently *Coffin Honey* and *Native Species*, both published by Michigan State University Press. He has won the Midwest Book Award, the Foreword INDIES Book of the Year Bronze and Silver Awards, the Gwendolyn Brooks Poetry Prize, the Chautauqua Editors Prize, and the Bloomsburg University Book Prize. He is an emeritus fellow of the Black Earth Institute and teaches environmental studies at Pennsylvania State University's Altoona College.

Kacie England is from Jacobus, Pennsylvania. She holds two bachelor's degrees, one in English Literature and another in Secondary Education: English, from Bloomsburg University of Pennsylvania, where she was also the 2020 recipient of the Baillie Award for the Critical Essay. Currently residing in Greencastle, PA, she teaches English literature and composition courses and advises campus publications at Mercersburg Academy, an independent, coed college-preparatory boarding and day school for secondary students and postgraduates.

Michael Garrigan writes and teaches along the Susquehanna River in Pennsylvania. He is the author of two poetry collections—*River, Amen* and *Robbing the Pillars*—and his writing has appeared in *Orion Magazine, The Hopper Magazine*, and *North American Review*. His work has been nominated for Best of the Net and The Pushcart Prize. He was the 2021 Artist in Residence for The Bob Marshall Wilderness Area and he believes every watershed should have a Poet Laureate. You can read more of his work at www.mgarrigan.com.

Crissandra George is the Digital Collections Librarian at Case Western Reserve University. She has a B.A. in Linguistics and Spanish with a minor in Swahili from the University of Mississippi. Additionally, she has an MA in Linguistics (2022) and an MA in Library and Information Science (2023) from the University of Kentucky. Her roots in PA have always played and continue to play a huge role in her research and career. Her current research focuses on how language, place, and history shape society around us, where she creatively incorporates innovative technological methods to compile and analyze datasets from historical collections.

Born in North Carolina, **Jimmy Guignard** teaches at Commonwealth University of Pennsylvania on the Mansfield campus. He wrote *Pedaling the Sacrifice Zone: Teaching, Writing, and Living above the Marcellus Shale*. North-central Pennsylvania reminds him of the North Carolina mountains, though with more bears and bald eagles and fewer barbecue joints.

Lilace Mellin Guignard lives in Wellsboro with her husband and two kids. A former teacher of creative writing, outdoor recreation leadership, and women's studies at Commonwealth University-Mansfield, she is now associate editor and publisher of *Mountain Home* magazine. Her memoir *When Everything Beyond the Walls Is Wild: Being a Woman Outdoors in America* came out in 2019 from Texas A&M University Press. Her poetry has appeared in *Northern Appalachia Review* and *Poetry* magazine, among others. In addition to hunting, she enjoys paddling her pack canoe and pretending she's Nessmuk (look him up). She wishes she could get the hang of fishing.

Originally from Los Angeles, **Michael Hardin** lives in Danville, Pennsylvania, with his wife and two children and teaches English at Wilkes University. He is the author of a poetry chapbook, *Born Again*, from Moonstone Press (2019), has had poems and creative nonfiction published in *Seneca Review*, *Connecticut Review*, *North American Review*, *Quarterly West*, among others, and has been nominated for a Pushcart.

Alison Condie Jaenicke is Assistant Director of Creative Writing at Penn State University, where she teaches writing. Born in Westmoreland County, PA, Alison was raised in the Washington, DC, area; earned her BA and MA in English at the University of Virginia; and lived for a time in Knoxville, TN. Since 2001, she's been settled back in her birth state. Alison's essays and stories have appeared in *Pleiades*, *Appalachian Review*, *Superstition Review*, and other places. Her essay "I Slept Well If You Slept Well," was recognized as Notable in *The Best American Essays 2016*. (https://alisoncjaenicke.weebly.com/)

Rachel Kesselman was born and raised in Northeastern Pennsylvania. She has lived in Paris for over a decade, where she writes and teaches. Her work has appeared in *Appalachian Review* and was a finalist for the Terry Tempest Williams Prize and Santa Fe Writers Project Literary Awards. An alumna of Bryn Mawr College and the Sorbonne, she is currently pursuing a Master of Studies in Creative Writing at the University of Oxford and acts as Workshop Director at La Muse Artists and Writers Retreat in the South of France.

Leonard Kress grew up in and around Philadelphia. Studied religion at Temple, Creative Writing at Columbia, and Polish at Jagiellonian University in Krakow, Poland. Published poetry, fiction, and translations in *Massachusetts Review, Iowa Review, American Poetry Review, and Harvard Review*. Seven poetry collections: *Living in the Candy Store and Other Poems*, *Walk Like Bo Diddley*, and *The Orpheus Complex, Craniotomy Sestinas,* and *Poppy Seeds.* Also a translation of the 19th century Polish Romantic epic, *Pan Tadeusz* by Adam Mickiewicz. Awarded three Individual Artist Fellowships in poetry and playwriting from the Pennsylvania Council on the Arts.

Claire Lawrence is a Professor of Creative Writing at Bloomsburg University with a PhD in Creative Writing Fiction from the University of Houston and an MFA in Fiction from the University of Utah. She has published fiction, poetry, and memoir in numerous magazines including *Crab Orchard Review, TriQuarterly, Event Magazine, Terra Nova, Western Humanities Review*, *Lunch Ticket* and *Juked.* She lives in the forest with her husband, children, and two Pekingeses named Mushu and Kung Pao.

Shu-Jiang Lu is an associate professor of English at the University of Pittsburgh at Greensburg where she teaches writing and literature. She has written on modernist poetry and on Asian / African American / World literature. Her work appeared in *Paideum*, the *CAALS* volume series, *South Central Review*, and *Critical Insights*. Lu's publications also include the translation of the novel *The Color Purple* by Alice Walker and a book of memoir *When Huai Flowers Bloom* (SUNY Press, 2007).

Professor Emeritus, *Presence* assistant editor, and WPSU *Poetry Moment* host, **Marjorie Maddox** has published 16 collections of poetry—including *How Can I Look It Up When I Don't Know How It's Spelled?* (Kelsay); *Seeing Things* (Wildhouse); *Transplant, Transport, Transubstantiation* (Yellowglen Prize); *Begin with a Question* (International Book and Illumination Book Awards); Shanti Arts ekphrastic collaborations *Heart Speaks, Is Spoken For* (with Karen Elias) and *In the Museum of My Daughter's Mind* (with Anna Lee Hafer)—as well as a story collection, 4 children's books, and *Common Wealth: Contemporary Poets on Pennsylvania* and *Keystone* (co-editor with Jerry Wemple). www.marjoriemaddox.com

Abby Minor lives in the ridges and valleys of central Pennsylvania, where she works on poems, essays, gardens, and projects exploring regional and reproductive politics. Her first book, *As I Said: A Dissent* (Ricochet Editions, 2022), is a collection of long documentary poems concerning abortion, justice, and citizenship in U.S. history. Granddaughter of Appalachian tinkerers and Yiddish-speaking New Yorkers, she teaches poetry in her region's low-income nursing homes, volunteers with the internationally active group Abortion Conversation Projects, and co-directs an arts education nonprofit called Ridgelines Language Arts. In 2018 she was awarded Bitch Media's Writing Fellowship in Sexual Politics.

Bathsheba Monk is the author of seven novels (one a *Chicago Tribune* Best Book of the Year), two artist biographies, a rhyming picture book, a musical and four plays. She received a cultural grant for playwriting from Massachusetts where she attended grad school. She was born in Bethlehem, PA, joined the army, traveled the world, got an education—real and theoretical—and now lives in Allentown, PA with her husband, Paul Heller. She founded Blue Heron Book Works which publishes memoirs and novels and plays—thirty-eight to date—as well as offering author editing, coaching, and ghostwriting services.

Matt Perakovich is a writer, artist, and editor living in Bloomsburg, Pa.

PJ Piccirillo is the author of the novels *The Indigo Scarf* and *Heartwood*, and the collected novella and stories *Nunc Stans—A Ferry Tale*. He has twice won the Appalachian Writers Association Award for Short Fiction. PJ is a literary artist-in-residence for the Pennsylvania Council on the Arts. An advocate of northern Appalachia's under-recognized literature, he has worked to build a name for its writers by founding the Writers Conference of Northern Appalachia (WCoNA) and the *Northern Appalachia Review*. PJ holds an MFA from the University of Southern Maine and a BA in English from Saint Francis University.

Steve Schneible is a lifelong Pennsylvanian and writer living & working in Philadelphia, Pennsylvania, where he lives with his wife. When not working as a science writer, Steve writes short fiction and essays.

Nick Stanovick is a writer and educator from the Pocono Mountains. He is an alumnus of Temple University, Auburn University, and CUNY Queens College. An International Poetry Slam Champion and the winner of the Robert Hughes Mount Jr. Prize, his work has appeared in *Nashville Review*, *Vinyl*, *The Academy of American Poets*, *Ghost City Review*, and *Crab Creek Review* among others.

Elizabeth Tussey is a writer and genealogist from Salem, Ohio. She is a graduate of the NEOMFA Consortium and her poetry and prose are featured and forthcoming in *I Thought I Heard a Cardinal Sing: Ohio's Appalachian Voices, Women of Appalachia Project, Horrifying Children: Hauntology, Barn Owl Review, The Encyclopedia of LBGTQIA+ Portrayals in American Film, Horror Homeroom,* and *Postcolonial Text*. Elizabeth's ancestors came to Pennsylvania during the 1600s and she has had a lifelong fascination with their stories as well as the history of the region. She currently lives in Coraopolis, Pennsylvania with her partner, Cooper.

About the Editors

Anne Dyer Stuart's publications include *NELLE, Pleiades, North American Review, AGNI, The American Journal of Poetry, Raleigh Review, Cherry Tree, Sugar House Review, The Texas Review, Louisiana Literature, New World Writing Quarterly*, and *The Louisville Review*. Her work won a Henfield Prize, *New South Journal*'s Prose Contest, was anthologized in *Best of the Web*, and nominated for *Best New Poets*. *What Girls Learn*, a finalist for *Comstock Review's* Chapbook Contest, was published by Finishing Line Press. She is professor of English and Creative Writing at the Bloomsburg campus of Commonwealth University of Pennsylvania.

A Pennsylvania native, **Jerry Wemple** is a poet, nonfiction writer, and editor. One line of his family has came to Pennsylvania in 1738 and has lived near Danville since the 1780s. He has published four poetry collections, mostly recently *We Always Wondered What Became of You* from Broadstone Books. He also co-edited, with Marjorie Maddox, two anthologies of poetry about Pennsylvania. Among Wemple's honors are the Naomi Long Madgett Poetry Award, a Pennsylvania Council on the Arts Fellowship in Literature, the *Word Journal* Chapbook Prize, a Vermont Studio Center Fellowship, and the Jack and Helen Evans Endowed Faculty Fellowship. His work has appeared in numerous journals and anthologies. He also served seven years in the US Navy and was a newspaper reporter in Massachusetts. Wemple is a Professor of English and Creative Writing at the Bloomsburg campus of Commonwealth University.

www.ingramcontent.com/pod-product-compliance
Lightning Source LLC
Chambersburg PA
CBHW010729270326
41930CB00018B/3417

* 9 7 9 8 8 8 8 1 9 3 0 4 4 *